Praise for Leadership Dash

Once I started reading Dr. Williams' book, I couldn't put it down. Her challenge to create and optimize leadership equity is a welcomed expansion to the collective thought on effective leadership. Dr. Williams clearly defines such leadership qualities as: influence, relationship building, personal growth and professional calling, and she shapes them for effective appropriation and implementation for the leadership process. Her poignant testimonies and engaging illustrations assist in communicating many truths and dispelling many myths about leadership. Dr. Williams' book is both a proven postulation and relevant submittal that will enhance the quality and improve the work of anyone who holds, or aspires to hold, any position of leadership.

Rev. Dr. James F. Miller, Pastor, DuPage AME Church, Lisle, IL
Chairman, Reach, Inc.

I am impressed by the depth and breadth of Dr. Williams' analysis of a complex yet simple concept—leadership. She has an uncanny ability to instruct and guide in a clear and concise manner while simultaneously exploring the intricacies of various aspects of leadership. I found myself questioning my own leadership capabilities, my connectivity and authenticity, my intent. The 12 meditations are thought provoking and inspirational—this book is absolutely a must read for anyone who considers themselves a leader of any kind.

Hon. Patricia Brown Holmes (ret), Chicago, IL

Excellent strategies for delivering maximum positive impact in the limited time we have been given at home, at work, and on earth. Dr. Williams' book provides insightful spiritual grounding for aspiring leaders in any organization or at any stage of development. This is a lively and energetic road map to self-improvement at any level.

M. Taylor Florence, Attorney and Counselor at law
Chairman, Bullivant Houser Bailey, Sacramento, CA

Taking an assessment of who you are at your core and how that drives your leadership abilities is a necessity for anyone interested in becoming a better leader. *Leadership Dash* takes you on an introspective and systematic journey that will improve you and your leadership acumen. Whether you are a seasoned leader, new leader or interested in becoming a leader, *Leadership Dash* is the book for you. I've taken the *Leadership Dash* journey and have unequivocally become a better leader because of it. Are you ready to make the most of your Leadership Dash?

Gabrielle Cummings, Hospital Vice President, Greater Chicago

Dr. Williams gets at the heart and art and ethics of how people become leaders of influence—leaders who leave a legacy. This book is not a quick and easy shortcut to success. It is a pathway for those who are ready to serve others, "stand in the gap for someone else," and "speak on behalf of those who are unable to speak for themselves." Dr. Williams provides tools for an intentional journey of call, vision, mission, and love. She offers meditations that can lead to self awareness, other awareness, and God awareness. If you are looking for a way to recognize, evaluate, and develop your life's purpose, here is a voice and companion to cheer you along the way.

Rev. Adele Calhoun, Co-Minister
Redeemer Community Church, Needham/Wellesley MA.
Author of Handbook of Spiritual Disciplines (IVP)
and Invitations from God (IVP)

For everyone who reads *Leadership Dash*, a door will open and a pathway will come into view. As you digest its wisdom, you will be urged to ask deep and honest questions of yourself, and you will be invited to enter into a place of reformation that leads to transformation. Each step of your journey with this author is worth it because Dr. Williams will provide you access to the virtues and principles necessary to become the "legacy leader" you were created to be, and she will show you the integral connections between your power, purpose, path, and plan. Dr. Williams has provided her readers a pathway to enhance and extend their personal leadership dash. All who follow will be changed, and those whom they lead will be blessed.

Rev. Dr. Zina Jacque, Pastor
Community Church of Barrington, Barrington, IL
Founder, Trinity Church Boston Counseling Center, Boston, MA.

In a world that promotes a "dancing through life" mentality, Dr. Williams reminds us that leaders are called to a deeper relationship to those around us. To embrace the lessons of *Leadership Dash* is to recognize that true leadership is not based upon what we can do TO others but is instead based upon what we do FOR others. Leaders who follow the selfless lessons of the "Dash" will identify evidence of their leadership and create a legacy which will go on and on and on.

David Whitehurst, Attorney and Counselor at law
Founding Partner, Whitehurst & Cawley, Dallas, TX

Leadership Dash is a terrific read. It is an inspiring, insightful, and informative book for current and future leaders. From a simple dash, Dr. Williams gives some creative gems, captures the true essence of leadership, and provides leaders with tremendous truths on how to live a life with meaning and significance.

Bishop Gregory G.M. Ingram, Presiding Prelate, AME Church
10th Episcopal District, Dallas, TX

Leadership
DASH

Leadership
DASH

BREAKING THROUGH THE FINISH LINE

GENEACE WILLIAMS, J.D., PH.D.

FOREWORD BY DOUGLAS R. SHARP, PH.D.

OUR LIVING WORD COMMUNICATIONS, INC.
an Illinois Company

Published by Our Living Word Communications, Inc.
Printed by Malloy, Inc.

Media Contact:
Stephanie Johnson, Proven Results, LLC.
sjohnson@provenresultsllc.com

Cover Design by James Arneson Art and Design (Jaad)
Book Layout and Design by PixelGraphics
Editing by Megan Markanich

This title may be purchased in bulk for educational, business, or religious use. For information, please e-mail inquiries to info@livingwaterforleaders.net

Book Categories: 1. Leadership. 2. Leadership development. 3. Executive Leadership/Development. 4. Spirituality and Leadership. 5. Inspirational. 6. Legacy. 7. Business. I. Title

ISBN 978-0-9829616-0-5-

Library of Congress Control Number: 2010938604

Printed in the United States of America

www.livingwaterforleaders.net

Dedication

This book is dedicated to the loving memory of my dad, Otha L. Williams, Sr., who was the first leader in my life. By the manner in which he lived and encouraged me to live, he taught me my leading principle—integrity. Through his untiring service to God and his dedication to his wife and the resulting family, I learned the true meaning of living a relational and connected life. His tireless commitment to the work of his hands led me on the journey that has ultimately produced the book you now hold in your hands. Thank you, Dad! You have given me so much that I will never be able to express it all. And as you so often said, "I'm running to make 100 because 99 and $\frac{1}{2}$ just won't do."

ACKNOWLEDGMENTS

Having now authored a book geared to teach, it is critically important for me to acknowledge those in my life who have over the years taught me so much that has influenced who I am today. Really, there are too many to name, but I must acknowledge the few listed below:

To my beloved mother, Catherine Williams, who taught me the love of people.

To my family, who taught me the how-tos in giving and receiving love.

To my sister, Dr. Carline Williams Strong, who taught me the true meaning of faith.

To my cousin Reaneat Harper, an amazing woman of God, who in the face of tragedy taught me the true meaning of forgiveness.

To my cousins Marshall Sims Littleton, Mary Sims Johnson, Eddie Mae Sims Craddieth, Clara Sims McGruder, Dorothy Sims Draine, Myrtis Sims, Lillie Sims Jobe, Rachel Sims Cook, Yolanda Sims Griffin, and Georgia Sims, who taught me an amazing expression of love in sisterhood.

To my childhood teacher Lorraine Cornelius, who taught me at a very early age to give my best to whatever I put my hands.

To my college, law school, and lifelong friend, Honorable Patricia Brown Holmes (ret), who stared death in the face and taught me courage.

To Sherri Lynn Phillips, who taught me the joy in sacrifice.

To Kara Burrell Wright, who taught me the possibility in my own voice by giving me space to just "do me."

To Pamela Garmon Johnson, who taught me the gentleness of leadership.

To Stephanie Johnson and Gabrielle Cummings, who have given unselfishly into my life and in the process have taught me it really is more blessed to give than to receive.

To James D. Montgomery Sr., a brilliant attorney, who taught me a great deal about lawyering but even more about the art of problem solving.

To Rev. Dr. Frank Anthony Thomas, who shall always be my pastor and friend and the one from whom I learned true humility and the meaning in listening for the call of life and then walking in its honor.

To my friends and colleagues with whom I shared many years at New Faith Baptist Church and who taught me leadership principles by helping to provide a foundation for the work I do today.

To Dr. Stirling Culp, a tremendously gifted person and friend, who taught me the true meaning of excellence in service.

To Dr. Constantine Sandu, who taught me critical thinking at a whole new level.

To Lee Brower, Greg Maddox, and Bryan McDonald, who listened, supported, and offered quiet influence while simultaneously teaching me the power in connecting in community.

To Dr. Henry Young, Dr. Kenneth Vaux, and Dr. Douglas Sharp, the dream team, who taught me the language of scholars.

To Rev. Dr. James F. Miller, Rev. Lana Parks Miller, and my DuPage AME family, who have taught me true authenticity by giving me space to grow fully into my authentic self.

To Nabil Foster, Lela Johnson, Henry Pierce, Susette Lunceford, Debra Islam, Jodi Ablin, Robyn Alexander, Benee Brown, Joan Ruedel, Joan Harrell, Jasmin French, and Gabrielle Martinez, who taught me the possibilities inherent in digging deeper. Words are insufficient to thank you for your commitment to this project.

To Dr. Sandy Adell, who taught me the power in sharing knowledge.

To Pete and June Tameling, who have taught me community by exemplifying the truth in neighborly leadership.

To my "Sister Friend" Prayer Circle, who taught me victory by gathering on one accord and for one purpose.

To Inzafaye Scott, who gave birth to the idea for our prayer circle.

To Bridgette Halford Rasberry, from whom I have learned too many lessons to name, I would like to thank you for being on this journey with me and leading this project to success. Words are inadequate to express my heartfelt gratitude for ALL you have done. You have shown true commitment to that which you believe. In the process, I have learned the possibilities in my dash and the real meaning of "breaking through the finish line."

To Leo Rasberry, thank you for teaching me the power in kindness.

To the reviewers of *Leadership Dash* – – – –, I would like to thank you for teaching me grace in giving feedback.

Here is my chance to say thank you publicly! I love you all. Dr. G

CONTENTS

FOREWORD

A very wise man by the name of Socrates long ago said, "The unexamined life is not worth living." I think about this, and after a few moments I realize that Socrates was quite correct. If one passes through life without conscious examination of who one is and what one is doing and why, it is quite possible that the resulting life will have no greater significance than the fleeting scenery observed from a passing train.

The time when it is expected that one will be a passive nonparticipant is at a movie or play in a theater. Sports arenas and stadiums, on the other hand, are for nonparticipants who can and maybe even should be active in their nonparticipation. Life from day to day, especially in the venues where we interact with others, lead or follow them, nurture and support them, and cooperate for the accomplishment of some tasks and goals larger than ourselves—these are *not* the times to be either a passive *or* active nonparticipant. These are the times where we are required not only to show up with our game face but to step up with our A game. These are the times, both of great importance and small measure, where we are to give evidence of our interest and our character.

One other philosopher of antiquity who pondered this matter of an examined life and the formation of character is Aristotle. His views on ethics and the moral life are treated at great length in his book *The Nicomachean Ethics.* Unlike many people, ancient and modern, who think about "ethics" as a set of rules and a list of oughts that must govern us as we live, Aristotle conceived of ethics as a matter of developing character; how we conduct ourselves and how we relate to others is less a matter of keeping laws and rules and more a matter of duty to oneself for the simple reason that the task of human life was to become the best person one could possibly become. What is good and right and true from an ethical perspective, for Aristotle, was also good and right and true for a person.

Aristotle brought practicality to his ethics with the notion of virtue. For him, virtue is the quality of excellence in a person or thing; it is what makes it possible for a person or a thing to do what it is supposed to do. If pens are to write, then having ink is a virtue. If human beings are to love, then having resolve is a virtue. For Aristotle, becoming the best person one can become entailed practicing the virtues known as the excellences of character. Expressed differently, every individual has a character that is formed over time by the simple act of engaging in behaviors and activities repeatedly. Thus virtue is a habit, and character is its result. If you want to be a person of integrity, developing the virtue of honesty, then the thing to do, according to Aristotle, is to act honestly at all times and circumstances, and soon enough you will have become an honest person. As a habit, moral virtue is an inclination to choose to act in certain ways to the exclusion of others ways. In Aristotle's view, an individual cultivates a virtue and becomes virtuous not by following a set of predefined moral rules or civil laws but by engaging in virtuous acts as a matter of choice and, ultimately, as a matter habit.

There is yet another person from antiquity whose teachings are instructive at this point. He too had a lot to say about the examined life and the cultivation of virtuous habits, and His name is Jesus. From His Sermon on the Mount to the many parables of the kingdom of God, Jesus had much to say about the need to reflect on one's own loyalties and relationships with God and with others. Arguably, choosing to do to others what one would have others do to oneself is possible only following some self-reflection. The parable of the wise and foolish builders invites reflection on whether one is building wisely or foolishly and what the consequences are of each. Curiosity about which of the myriad commandments is the most important one can reflect a level of self-awareness intent on striving for excellence, but it can also reveal a wide but shallow level of commitment. Of all possible human responses, Jesus' ministry evoked in His hearers and followers the need to make choices, to discriminate between what is healthful and what is hurtful, what is honorable and what is shameful, what contributes to the wholeness of others and what diminishes their life. He encouraged and even cajoled those who followed Him to strive for excellence, to be all they could become by seeking first things first, and by knowing which things were truly first and which things followed. As odd as it may sound to our moralizing ears, Jesus commanded His followers to be *perfect* because the One who created them out of all-embracing love was *perfect*. Beyond cultivating virtuous habits and forming character, this command says this quite plainly: Be complete, as you are intended to be by the One who in the divine self is complete!

Now we all know that's easier said than done. Truth to tell, it sounds rather burdensome: If perfection is the goal, how reasonable and practical can the way there actually be? As it happens, Jesus had something to say about this too. It is possible to be complete, to be, as Aristotle put it, the best person one can possibly become but not without effort. As Jesus noted, taking the path of least resistance will not lead to excellence or virtue or completion or life or anything but self-destruction and the destruction of others. As interested as we are in the shortest routes and the fastest speedways, high speed limits and higher altitudes, the fact is that those intent on completion and perfection must take the path of greatest resistance, the one with the most obstacles, and the least even terrain. Jesus called this the narrow gate and the narrow road; Aristotle called it the good life of moral virtue.

The book you now hold in your hand is written with this narrow gate and narrow road in mind. Dr. Geneace Williams has spent more years than I care to count as a leader not just of others but of other leaders. The places where she has exercised this role are as local as a congregational facility or a corporate office and as global as the far-flung reaches of Latin America, Europe, and the Caribbean. As a result of her work and experience in all these places, she has cultivated the virtue of leadership so much so that it is not just something she does with others as a habit but it also embraces a strategy for training and equipping others to exercise leadership at a higher, more effective level. This book is thus about you, the reader, the one whose leadership journey may have been jerky or smooth but in either case one that has not yet fully expressed the virtuous character you seek to cultivate and has not yet achieved the impact you desire.

Plato and Aristotle and Jesus are pressing us to personal *reformation*. That's a word with which many of us are perhaps not comfortable. Dr. Williams now joins that chorus with the declaration that those in positions of leadership in social, corporate, and religious sectors would be well advised to do things differently by first becoming different persons. Herein lies the challenge and the threat. Wanting to be better at what we do is a positive thing, but having to change in order to achieve that is, by many, regarded as a negative thing. Dr. Williams argues that it doesn't have to be that way. Her challenge to you in this book is to ease into it by pausing just long enough over a brief period of time to increase your *self-awareness* (asking, Who am I, and who do I want to become?), reflect on your *convictions* (asking, What do I believe in, and is it really congruent with my work?), assess your *values* (asking, What is/are the most important matters and persons to me, the ones that most influence my choices?), and consider yet again the *strategies* you use to move forward (asking, What are my methods for defining and achieving both personal and professional goals?).

There is a kind of reciprocity between leadership and the circumstances in which it is exercised. To William Butler Yeats is attributed the saying: "Do not wait to strike till the iron is hot; but make it hot by striking." Whether circumstances produce leaders or leaders produce circumstances is a debate others can have. What interests Dr. Williams is *who* persons in leadership *are* and *what* they are competent to *do*. Hence her work here—especially in the meditations—focuses on living with leaders and leadership for a little while in a different way. Engaging her in the reading of this book will be cultivating leadership virtues, practicing them in an innovative way. Staying with her will put you in a position to assess your own resolve for excellence and invite you to perceive otherwise familiar situations quite differently. Most importantly, with Dr. Williams as your colleague, you will find empowerment to embrace a new, more enduring direction for your own life and leadership.

The mutuality at the heart of Dr. Williams' work here is the interpenetration of purpose, plan, and path, all coalescing in the power to become complete, the best person you can possibly become, the author of a fully examined and fully purposeful life. There should be no doubt about it: this will involve work, and many are they who are too faint of heart to carry it through. But for those who endure, there is the promise of setting out on truly a journey to greatness, a pathway that will impact others and cultivate your own reformation. So let the journey begin!

by Douglas R. Sharp, Ph.D.

I

Preparing for
the Race

Chapter 1

THE FIRST WORD

If you are anything like me, when you discovered this book you were attracted to and interested in its title and what it could possibly mean in your life. Moreover, if you are like most people with whom I have spoken, you are probably thinking the title is a sports metaphor challenging you as a leader to dash like a champion sprinter to your leadership finish line. In actuality, the title of this work carries a double entendre, and the sports analogy is simply one interpretation. My aim in titling this work, however, is to challenge you and cause you to dig deeper. Consequently, at the outset, I invite you to strap on your thinking cap. You will need it—beginning with the title.

So here it is: Many years ago I was asked a very profound question. However, as I sit writing this manuscript I cannot for the life of me recall by whom. Yet this very pregnant question redirected my life. In short, I was asked, What are you doing with your dash? The questioner was referring to the en dash (–) that is often used to separate a person's year of birth and year of death. As an example, the mark utilized between these two years (1920–1993) has been referred to as a dash. Metaphorically, the dash represents your life's work and the actual contributions you make during your lifetime. Truthfully, it is possible to offer insignificant as well as significant, negative as well as positive, small as well as great, passive as well as active, idle as well as transforming, short-lived as well as intergenerational contributions. The decision is left in the hands of the contributor.

In this personal experience enumerated above, I came to understand my questioner was challenging me to think more critically about the ways in which I was spending my time—translated—my life on earth. Thankfully, the question prompted me to a new level of thinking about my life's journey as well as the legacy God had placed me on earth to fulfill. What impact was I having? What contributions was I making? What was I doing that was really worthwhile? Was it all about attaining the notable title, amassing wealth, having a global name known by untold numbers of people, living in the right neighborhood, shopping in the right places, and driving the acceptable automobile? Could there really be something more to this thing called life?

In all honesty, I must admit I had decided on another title for this book, but toward the end of completion I was redirected to this very profound question, and the title

Leadership Dash – – – – was revealed to me. The subtitle, on the other hand, was a last-minute gift inspired by a vision I received while contemplating the joy I was to experience in the victory of seeing this project published. So as I open this work, I feel compelled to ask you this question: What are you doing with your leadership dash?

With that said, if the title of this book tempts you to focus only on your individual accomplishments or on the road to attaining your next leadership accolade, consider yourself challenged to think again. This work is meant to prompt you as a leader to re-consider your paradigm about what it means to be a great leader. It is, in effect, a challenge in the form of a leadership "call to action." That is, life is calling; the action step is up to you.

Interestingly, while penning this work, another friend asked me whether or not leadership could be wholly defined and if it is really possible for anyone to know, in fact, if one has led well. In retrospect, perhaps my friend has raised valid questions. And while it may not be possible to capture leadership from every perspective, this work asserts there are certain virtues and principles of leadership that are essential in the process of achieving legacy, and the theories espoused herein are based on these important virtues and principles.

So allow me to begin with some basics about leaders and leadership. Before doing so, however, I must make a confession. When I began this project, I was convinced I had uncovered the true definition of leadership, but toward the end of the writing process the definition I had been living with for a long time prior thereto changed. In keeping with my experience, I shall begin this work with my original definition of leadership. And just as it happened to me, I will share my new definition of leadership near the end of this work. Simply stated, as we begin this journey together I would like you to be aware of the change that occurred in me during the course of writing this book. Now having made such a confession, let us turn to my initial definition.

Leadership is the art of ethically influencing others to move toward a particular goal or specific achievement and is marked by intentionality and an attitude of service. It is a term of action, and true leaders are developed by the actions to which they commit. Be assured that genuine leadership is not about having the power to tell someone else what to do, your ability to hold the attention of an audience, the impact you have made to the company's bottom line, or the size of your last bonus or client contract. Genuine leadership is also not about altering the lives of others in a negative direction for your own personal gain. To the contrary, reaching the mark of an authentic and influential leader is defined by your capacity to impact the lives of others in a positive direction—one that leaves them better for having had an encounter with you. Your greatness depends on how well you learn to serve the needs of others, particularly those to whom justice has yet to be served. Your greatness is defined by your resolve to stand in the gap for someone else and your willingness to speak on behalf of those who are unable to speak for themselves. In fact, true leadership is measured by your power to exercise the gift of love, your willingness to walk in service, humility, self-understanding and integrity, and your motivation toward intentionality— "come what may."

The idea of legacy leadership is most critical to this writing. Legacy, as I contend, is a goal to which the greatest leaders strive. With legacy, as will be discussed in Chapter 4, one contemplates becoming the kind of leader who works to create a lasting, positive impact in the lives of others. It is the kind of impact that will cause them to also be equipped to offer great contributions to our global community. For that reason, this writing prompts several questions: On what path are you traveling? Are you on a quest for leadership or a pathway to legacy? Are you motivated by a value-driven system energized by the purpose for which your life was created? Have you heard and answered your life's call?

As a longtime lawyer, former corporate legal executive, student of social justice theory, spiritual advisor, entrepreneur, and now author, I have enjoyed the privilege of experiencing leadership in the many different facets of my professional life. Most know me as lawyer, yet some are acquainted with me as ardent student and advocate of critical legal theory and theology. Others still have come to know me as clergy, confidant, and spiritual advisor while those most recently making my acquaintance are getting to know me as entrepreneur and author. Notwithstanding the phase of professional and leadership development in which I have found myself, I have learned tremendous lessons about the joys and challenges associated with the title "leader."

I have learned what great leaders do *and* what great leaders refuse to do. I have learned the remarkable interconnectedness between values lived and value added while also discovering the profound correlation between leadership, values, and justice.[1] I have learned life speaks, and it speaks whether or not we are prepared to take note. I have learned the importance of silencing chaos and noise in order to listen attentively to hear life and what it is saying about the path and pathway to personal purpose and true legacy leadership. Most critical, in my diverse and very fortunate professional career, I have learned one thing remains constant: People from all walks of life desire authentic and transforming leadership. At the same time, there is a present-day crisis in leadership and what it means and does not mean to chart the course toward legacy leadership. As one with a very long history of inconspicuously and introspectively studying people, I have come to understand that while people desire leadership they desire a different kind of leadership than that of yesterday. They desire something different than "the way we have always done it here."

Thus in this writing you will be challenged to consider what I call an old form of leadership versus a more contem-

---

[1]In this writing, the term *justice* understands life to be relational and translates into living an intentional, integrated, and connected life in whatever venue one finds oneself. In this writing, social justice refers to collective efforts to build a social order that favors the many instead of the few and, for me, is considered an ideological and theological imperative.

plative ideology about authentic leadership. I maintain the old form of leadership is individual (self-centered), directional (demanding), and billable (driven by monetary gain) against a newer ideology of leadership that is relational (other-centered), connectional (community-minded), and sacrificial (servant-driven). The fact is people desire real relationships with real people who honor integrity, honesty, open communication, authenticity, transparency, acceptance, mutual respect, and care and concern. Most profound, I have learned from the remnants and ashes of life's experiences (both good and challenging) come wisdom as the forerunner to realizing truth and authenticity reside in leadership; or even better, legacy leadership resides at the core of truth and authenticity.

Ironically, I have come to learn many leaders desire to be great architects of their lives as leaders but unfortunately have not enjoyed the success that is commonly associated with legacy leadership. Perhaps the answer can be uncovered in this simple truth: Leadership is common, but legacy is not all so common. Nonetheless, the term *leadership* has become commonplace and the buzz word of today. The truth is, however, as leaders we have a great deal of work yet to do.

I have learned what many leaders have about lasting change: Systemic revolution is a long and arduous task not given to the swift or the strong. The greatest leadership lesson I learned while penning this book has become a profound teaching in my own life: We spend far too much time chasing purpose instead of moving to a place where we can hear and respond to life's call, which for each of us is uniquely our own.

My own journey in leadership has taught me that every great leader both desires and requires encouragement and renewal for the journey that is theirs to travel. The pathway, which is often uncharted, may be isolated, lonely, and difficult. Although often unspoken, leaders themselves also need inspiration accompanied by a nudge or push to keep them on the path of growth and continued self-development. Complacency is a word that belongs outside the purview of a leader's vocabulary. When a bona fide leader grows, space is created for further growth in those who follow. That kind of leader understands success is measured by the stride of those who have been chosen to pick up their mats and follow. More important, genuine leaders have uncovered the authentic nature of leadership in giving and living in service to others. In simple terms, in all of my years as leader, I have come to understand the critical nature of grounding leadership in a steward-driven theology and ideology of service. At day's end, life's best is created from our greatest place of service.

Hence this project was inspired by my own journey on the road to finding my greatest leadership contribution— a legacy of helping others navigate their way through the liminal periods of life or the times between where they sit almost as onlookers before embracing the place to which they are being summoned to stand and live. In short, this book is a contribution to the body of work dedicated to leadership and leadership development. Its angle is slightly different. Here I take the liberty of combining substantive work predicated on the interconnectedness of experiential formation and a theory on "legacy mapping" together with the fundamentals of an Integrity-Based Leadership Model (IBLM). Practically speaking, I also include a discussion of the SAAG Principle: Setting and Achieving Goals. SAAG is a practical and achievable development process designed to help leaders learn the art of letting go. Learning to let go at an organic and authentic level is a key factor in not only achieving lasting results but also in making room for continued growth. I conclude with twelve leadership meditations geared to help readers on the road to recovering and discovering the connection between true and authentic leadership and their life's inward journey.

If legacy is a goal to which you truly aspire, take time to understand the challenges outlined in this work and the principles set forth herein. It is key to appreciate from the outset that legacy must be divorced from you. Legacy concerns itself with others. As such, be prepared to confront yourself at a new level of depth through critical thought and self-reflection. In other words, be prepared to consciously examine who you are, what you are doing, and whether or not you are being called in a different direction. Your profession or level really does not matter. Whether you are a spiritual leader, doctor, lawyer, corporate executive, business leader, entrepreneur, educator, financial executive, public service leader, nonprofit leader, or even aspiring leader, this work was written with you in mind. So take this leadership journey and be encouraged and challenged on your own voyage to greater leadership depth. Along the journey, begin to internalize the leadership principles and actions discussed in this work. They are sure to make a tremendous difference in your *Leadership Dash* – – – –. My aim is singular—to help leaders become more intentional with their – – – – by sharing on the road to creating and fulfilling legacy. In revealing what I have learned as a leader, I can only hope this work inspires you on your own pathway to greater leadership depth and provides a new level of oxygen for the journey that is ahead. That said, join me on this journey, but remember that your results are up to you indeed!

Chapter 2

A LEGACY BREAKTHROUGH: FORMATION AS FOUNDATION

Formation is the first critical message of this writing and the underpinning for the entire work—that is, formation is a necessary element on the pathway to becoming the brand of leader whose leadership carries a lasting and positive impact on both the professional and personal lives of others. In simple terms, formation is the reconstruction of you into the person you were intended to be. So you ask, what are you saying? It's simple; I believe you were uniquely created to achieve a distinct purpose that begins with formation. Therefore, we will spend this chapter unpacking the true meaning behind what is meant by formation. It suffices to say at the outset, however, embarking upon true leadership is a journey, and great leaders grow into their best selves often through life lessons associated with mistakes made and corresponding growth and maturity. Just ask the next

CEO you meet if he or she has made any mistakes while serving in their capacity as chief executive officer. I can almost guarantee the universal answer will be absolutely. Truthfully, the leader who has not grown and matured from experience, including mistakes made, is either not very effective as a leader or living in a state of denial.

In essence, leaders are formed, and the work of formation is accomplished at the deepest levels of experience. In other words, the road to legacy begins in the trenches of formation. Think of formation as foundational; just as a builder would not attempt to build a home on sand so it is in life. Your legacy as a leader must begin with a solid foundation. It must begin with the process of formation. Intentionality around formation better prepares you for the work of leading others. And in case you have not heard it before, I am happy to be the first to inform you that leadership is not about you. On the contrary, it is all about those you lead or serve. With that in mind, we turn to the journey of understanding formation and what it means for your life as a leader.

Dr. M. Scott Peck begins his book *The Road Less Traveled* with this simple phrase, "Life is difficult."[2] One of the many reasons life may be difficult for you as a leader relates to the fact you are, whether consciously or unconsciously, consistently in a state of development. Truthfully leadership and growth go hand in hand, and the various stages of a life in leadership cause us to tug, pull, war,

---

[2] M. Scott Peck, M.D., The Road Less Traveled (New York: Simon & Schuster, 1978).

embrace, release, relinquish, and eventually become. Every experience, large or small, prompts and promotes action and reaction and is a contributor to formation. Every challenge or promotion (formal or informal) carries instruction that inspires or should inspire further growth and development. In fact, a leader whose aim is legacy must first recognize the critical nature in a process of formation. That process requires making a decision to become and fulfill that which you were created to achieve. Simply put, it is not a matter of wanting. Rather it is a matter of deciding and renewing, and renewing is at the core of difficult work.

You must renew your vision of who you are and where you are. You must renew your understanding of where you have been and what you have accomplished; you must also be prepared to take up new challenges—especially if you have not discovered your true calling in life. While it is true you cannot go back over old territory, you can start every day anew on the road to being formed into the person your life intends. It begins with a belief you are destined to achieve a life's call that is much greater than you can accomplish single-handedly and without the benefit of formation.

As referenced in this work, formation is a kind of reformation that concludes in transformation. And true transformation is made possible when a leader develops the confidence to overcome obstacles, the internal fortitude to face fears and conquer strongholds, the courage to walk in uncharted territory, the determination to defeat destruction, the ability to avoid derailment, the wherewithal to defy deterrence, the gift to discern the detour, and the know-how to deny the enemy. In other words, formation is serious business that requires you to abandon comfort for tough internal work that promises to challenge your thinking and prepare you to operate at a different level. You will know you are ready for formation work when you are equipped to confront the possibilities that exist beyond your level of comfort and are willing to embrace the fact that positive change presupposes confronting your growing edges. Likewise, the leader who desires authentic and transforming growth is primed to resist the temptation to remain or become anesthetized by life's challenges and/or its successes. Instead they are motivated to move as if life itself is depending on their willingness to pursue the journey of formation.

Formation is a moral imperative both in life and leadership. As such, true formation work is a prompter inviting you down the path of setting values and ethical boundaries by which you will live and lead. It is a dynamic, continual process fueled by receipt of input and feedback, both internal and external, and it requires responding in an active manner. In essence, it is a journey that occurs over time.

In this work, I contend true formation happens at the point of intersection between intentionality and authenticity.[3] Intentional leaders concern themselves with who they are and the path they travel. An authentic leader is genuine beyond the surface and ever seeking her true self

---

[3] Intentionality and authenticity are discussed at greater length in Chapter 5.

while working to live a purposed life shaped by a personal philosophy of integrity. With crucial ties to integrity, moral consciousness and ethical patterns are the rules of law in formation. Said another way, rules of law are standards and boundaries by which one chooses to live, and the work of formation suggests integrity, honesty, morality, virtue, honor, and service. In fact, ethical formation is a personal, values-based system of principles by which a great leader chooses to live and operate, and an ethical mode of operation is an essential in the lives of leaders. In that way, it is individual inside-out work that develops, shapes, changes, refines, reforms, transforms, molds, and prepares. Unlike external work, which is temporal, true formation work is work that lasts, as the internal is infinite. In other words, true formation is transforming and transformative. It is an outgrowth of a continual and critical model of self and life reflection that will provide you an opportunity to learn as well as grow. In short, the greatest leaders understand they are shaped for the better by life's experiences—something I term *experiential formation*.

Experiential formation teaches experience is life's greatest instructor. But experience can be the best teacher only when we learn the lesson an experience was designed to teach. Nothing happens in life apart from experience. Often whether young or more mature we become our experience—good, bad, or indifferent. The fact is, experience shapes, forms, and reforms, and life is made up of a series of experiences. While you cannot always control your experience you can control how you respond. As a leader, it is a critical imperative to understand we each experience a life occurrence in our own manner. Therefore, the way in which you experience a particular event may be very different than the experience of others. The important matter is to understand these differences and to appreciate your experience while consciously and deliberately determining the ways in which you will allow the experience to shape you and, therefore, your response.

One of the many experiences you may encounter as a leader undergoing formation involves what may feel like moments of exile. Do not define yourself by your exile, but understand that your response while in exile will characterize you. Be assured that wilderness moments are temporary. Wisely use your time to traverse the rough places in ways that foster and encourage listening, learning, and growing. Do not fret during instances of perceived silence by your God, or that in which you believe, as intimacy with your God will teach you the language of silence. Understand the power, meaning, and depth of transformation that is often communicated in the whispers of the quiet, and avoid the temptation to run, sprint, jog, or dart from the very idea of spending time alone. Rather, comprehend the value that is gained for your journey during the quiet and time of reflection.

It is true that everyone does not place the same premium value on experience, which suggests there are those who have not learned to evaluate their experiences against outcomes in their lives. Yet I advocate evaluating life experiences as well as how you respond to them as a means of better understanding behaviors, patterns, growth (or lack thereof), and opportunities for further development in your walk as a leader. The result, I hope, will be that you come to appreciate that wise leaders use their experience as a catalyst for growth and development. They understand the value in lessons learned and turn tragedies into triumphs and testimonies to encourage others on their own roads of life. In other words, they leverage experience for a greater good and view the setback as a setup allowing them the opportunity to operate in an even greater space and pave the way for exponential impact. Unfortunately, absent close assessment, experiences are often repeated because the intended lesson has gone uninterpreted. The value of experience can often be gained only through close and critical examination. Even more important, the greatest leaders allow their life experiences to aid as they become greater contributors in the lives of others.

One experience I have repeated many times as a leader involves my sincere desire to "mine" the gifts in others to bring them to their fullest potential. My former approach was the same or very similar with each person with whom I was working. My approach was to continually and strongly encourage them to achieve at the level of excellence while simultaneously and frequently increasing their responsibility. My style of feedback was straightforward and to the point, as I desired to be honest with others. (After all, that is how I preferred that others deal with me.) What I learned from the experience over many years was that not everyone wanted to be pushed to their fullest potential, and not everyone wanted straightforward, honest, and sometimes critical feedback. The lesson I was fortunate to learn was the art of dealing with each person I led from the perspective of the particular person in question. That experience certainly helped me reach the place where I am today—a place of carefully assessing and understanding how to reach and impact each person with whom I interact right where they are. Not much that is great can be accomplished unless and until leaders learn to deal with an-other at that person's precise "point of contact." The level of effective communication is increased tremendously when you are able to authentically connect with an-other at their point of contact. And the point of contact involves clearly understanding and appreciating difference.

I am also reminded of another experience that aided in my formation. In my days of practicing law in a corporate environment, I had the privilege of providing leadership to hundreds of lawyers around the country as well as developing and sharing best practices, counsel, and advice with lawyers from around the world. I was determined to use the trust that had been placed in me to help others grow and achieve success in legal matters. I realized from the outset that the opportunity I had been extended was not at all about me, so I worked tirelessly to bring value to the matters wherein others were looking to me for leadership. As a result, I gained great respect as an expert, and my sphere of influence broadened. From a formation perspective, it was the kind of experience that helped me mature in my ability to influence others while simultaneously remaining humble.

Yet another experience involves a friend who worked for me but who also knew me outside of the work environment. At the time, I thought it was important to leave Geneace the minister, teacher, spiritual advisor, "counselor," and African American woman at home instead of allowing her to accompany me to work. I wanted to be lawyerly, corporate, and professional, and I wanted to keep my life compartmentalized such that there would be no mistake about who I was while engaged in the practice of law. One day, however, my friend invited me to allow Geneace, in the whole of who I was, to come to work. He explained how people were missing out on the side of me that naturally drew others to want to learn and grow through my teaching. Now, of course, my friend was not inviting me to proselytize those who worked for me. Rather, he was inviting me to relax, let down my guard, and allow others to experience me in the fullness of the person I was and was created to be. He helped me to get comfortable with the idea of removing the masks and allowing the true me to come forth so that I could blossom and others could gain and learn from my years of experience and the wealth of knowledge and wisdom I had come to amass. Looking back, my dear friend was helping me with formation. At the time, however, I could not identify the process as such. Now, on the other hand, it is as clear as a bright, sunny day.

Now think of a challenging "leadership" experience in your life. Use it as your opportunity for critical, self-reflective thought, and develop a strategy that turns your experience into a beneficial outcome for you and others. Use it to help you in formation. I think the saying goes as follows: When life gives you lemons, make lemonade.

The level of critical thought and reflection I am suggesting in this work is akin to the learning method utilized in the training and development of lawyers. I vividly recall my law school experience where I was literally baptized in Socratic methodology. The Socratic Method, in short, employs a dialectical technique of critical discussion between instructor and students. The process is engaged to prompt the student to emerge as one who is capable of thinking and engaging at a more critical level. As such, the student is more apt to gain a greater ability to reason, critique multiple sides of an issue, increase his knowledge, and reach a conclusion based upon what has been gleaned through the process. There is, as I have learned from living the Socratic Method most of my adult professional life, something important that happens in the midst of critical thinking and dialogue. Simply stated, it promotes growth at greater levels of depth.

But perhaps you have not experienced Socratic methodology firsthand, or just maybe the Socratic Method analogy does not speak to you. Let's examine a slightly different illustration, which also speaks to the value of critical thinking. Consider the process of learning to swim, and then reflect upon the following: "great leaders avoid shallow water thinking." In swimming, the instructor starts his student in the shallow end. The shallow end experience is meant to help the student become less fearful of the unknown, more comfortable in the water as well as knowledgeable, and at ease with swimming technique. In essence, a student's time in the shallow end is designed to teach an important how-to lesson while simultaneously minimizing fear of launching into the deep. The shallow water is akin to "easy" because a swimmer can reduce risk and difficulty by simply changing his position to a stand.

In life, just as in swimming, there are those who have not allowed themselves the gift of release from shallow water thinking. Shallow water thinking limits one's imagination. It prevents you from moving beyond what is comfortable. It tempts you to continue with the things that offer little challenge and stimulus for growth. It leaves room for fear and doubt and edges out courage. In fact, it discourages you from pushing yourself to the next level of performance. It disavows you of faith and champion thinking and certainly limits your ability to accomplish what is beyond your immediate reach. I have often said "the potential for extraordinary becomes possible at the edge of comfort." And, yes, I am advocating marching right up to the edge of your comfort zone and letting go as if you were approaching the edge of a cliff prepared to jump. Be assured that if you have been faithful to your preparatory work the parachute of life is bound to open.

Consider a real life example. I think it is safe to say

Michael Phelps would have never become a champion Olympic swimmer had he remained in the shallow end. Instead, he allowed himself to grow and become a champion by thinking and ultimately launching into the deep. Moreover, I am certain he found it essential to surround himself with those who possessed deep water mentality rather than shallow water thinking. By doing so, he allowed himself to learn their way of thinking, their practices, as well as their training methods.

Using an example from Christendom, even while hanging on a cross Jesus maintained a Sunday morning victory mentality rather than a Friday evening attitude of defeat. In three days, His resurrection victory was won for all the world of believers to see. Thus, for those who believe, one could say Jesus did not suffer from shallow water thinking.

The same is true of legacy leadership. It happens outside of your comfort zone and requires you to launch into the deep. Regardless of your level of leadership, if your desire is to be a leader who creates legacy, you must move beyond the old familiar and take a step toward the unfamiliar, the challenging—that which is larger than you. In my own life, I have found it true that you take on the habits and character traits of those with whom you surround yourself. Thus, if you desire to expand your thinking and your growth, you must surround yourself with those who think at the level to which you aspire.

Notwithstanding, launching into the deep does not exempt you from sometimes feeling as if you are about to drown. It might happen that you take in a little water from time to time. Even the greatest of swimmers have had this experience. At those moments, instead of allowing fear to overtake you, it becomes critical for you to take up your lifeline and continue, which is precisely why it is important to surround yourself with those who think even more critically than you. (They will serve as your lifeline.) Moreover, the deep water was not meant to be overcome easily. It is meant to challenge you until you achieve more than you ever thought was possible. When you do revisit shallow water, it is not about returning to what is comfortable. Moreover, resist the temptation to surround yourself with shallow water thinkers. It will cause you to remain in the shallow end—thus missing your opportunity to launch into the deep. Parenthetically, launching into the deep does not mean you will never revisit the shallow end. When you return to the shallow end, however, it is because there is work to be done. There are those in the shallow end who need your assistance to launch into the deep. They need to learn the lesson you learned about courage and how to put courage to work in order to put fear to flight.

Applied to formation, critical thinking (deep water mentality) is a prompter that should lead you to ask, What are my growing edges, who do I want to become, what do I want to accomplish, who am I called to be, and what path must I travel? Formation also prompts the important question: Who do I not want to be? Without formation, it is not possible to achieve at authentic, transformative, transparent, influential, and impactful levels. With formation and critical thinking, a new level of clarity about your journey becomes possible. Moreover, and for certain, it is unlikely a leader will achieve legacy without clarity. Simply put, clarity is the place where one has attained an unmistakable and unambiguous understanding of the path he is to travel. Gaining clarity is unequivocally a part of the formation process. Further, formation is the beginning of legacy and in essence the starting block. Like a great runner if you fail to get into the starting block you will fail to get into the position of preparation. Lack of preparedness impedes progress on the journey to legacy. Even more critical, the more genuine and impactful the formation and critical thinking process, the more clarity becomes accessible.

While education and training are important components of professional development, values, character, integrity, morality, and humanity are vital parts that make up the inner person and are at the center of experiential formation. These character traits cannot be imposed from the outside in and cannot be applied to life by simply reading a book. Rather, they require building from the inside out. They are shaped by experience, critical thought, self-evaluation, feedback, mistakes, corrections, and continued development. The inner person determines strength of character and thus describes who one really is. Who one is authentically defines his true formation and ability to contribute at the level of legacy. As such, formation is first intrapersonal and second interpersonal. Intrapersonal work means I spend time understanding who I am from the inside out as well as learning the importance of reflecting upon areas within me that are ripe for personal growth. I learn to be self-aware and to engage in self-care. I learn that caring for self makes room for the care and concern of others. I learn it is neither masculine nor feminine to develop strong intrapersonal skills. Rather, it is a human imperative giving me room to grow in formation. Moreover, when a leader develops strong intrapersonal relations, he is better able to connect with community in an expression of interpersonal competence. Interpersonal competence allows a leader to help others realize their own life's call and the road toward its achievement. Interpersonal competence means I understand the value of approaching others in ways that respect who they are and where they are. It means I understand we each are different, and I appreciate the value in difference. I am able to empathize with others while maintaining a set of values and boundaries by which I live. I understand the importance of authenticity, transparency, and honesty in my dealings with others.

Formation denotes order. Thus, if you are lacking order in your life, perhaps it is time to revisit formation. True formation work will alter your life as well as your leadership journey. While formation is inside-out work, it is not work that can be accomplished absent outside stimulation. It requires outside input to help you understand what others see and experience as a result of an encounter with you. The outside encounter assists you in your ability to live life in a reflective manner. Its banner is an invitation to be made anew. You are invited to examine, reflect, take note, and understand your growing edges. Then you are called to begin the process of change management by moving proactively. Consider these questions: What shapes me, and what has shaped my path? Thereafter, consider the following image.

The work of formation is akin to a potter sitting before his wheel to create a piece of art. Think of yourself as clay and life as the potter who is prepared to mold and make you into the form life intends. Being on the potter's wheel means you allow yourself to become pliable. You willingly permit yourself to become an open vessel to cooperate in the work of the potter. Rigidity becomes a thing of the past, as you fully understand the plasticity of clay. It is capable of undergoing permanent reshaping and reforming in order to be transformed into the shape fashioned by its potter. Formation is finding the right path and direction and pursuing it with passion. Experiential formation is about your personal journey of becoming, and becoming is about your journey toward creating impact beyond your dash (finish line). It is not about your journey of working to form others. Personal work is always an important forerunner to public witness.

While formation is personal work, the process is not designed to be accomplished single-handedly and on your own. The potter leaves the process with very visible signs of having been at work. Like the image at the end of this chapter, his hands are full of the residue of clay and are tired from the molding process. His shoulders are bent forward and aching from the posture of creation. It reminds me of the process I endured as the potter of this book. Daily my hands were aching from hours before the computer. Daily my shoulders ached while leaning before my computer contemplating and writing in an effort to produce the best work of my life. When I began this process, I still believed writing my doctoral dissertation was my toughest creation process next to law school and the bar. But being the potter of this creation has become the most challenging of my professional life. And it has helped me understand the real level of commitment required during any process of formation.

If you desire to take seriously the work of formation, find an accountability partner, set realistic and attainable goals for yourself, regularly evaluate your progress with someone else, and consistently challenge yourself to achieve at the next level. Incidentally, if you are truly "called" to leadership, you must understand not everyone is meant to share the intimate details on the road you are destined to travel. Thus, in selecting an accountability partner, I encourage you to embark upon an expedition toward wisdom to discern who is meant to share your journey. Clearly define your moral and ethical boundaries and set a value system by which your life will be guided. Make a personal decision to live into your values regardless of what others may do. Remember that formation demands an extra measure of determination and a spirit of expectation. It will require a yearning for growth so much so that you commit to a life-changing regimen that places you on a course toward setting and achieving more challenging goals. What works for someone else may not work for you.

So you must get to know you and what it takes for you to continue growing no matter what.

Do not forget the necessity for a spirit of expectation. Move to a place where you expect change and growth in your life. Be prepared to navigate obstacles that may present themselves and tempt you not to work at becoming the best leader you could possibly become. You must be prepared to say yes to growth and *no* to the things that come to short-circuit your progress. You must also be unwavering in utilizing your experience to help guide you in determining the way to go and the way to avoid.

One of the first and most important questions in leadership formation relates to who you are called to be. Truly understanding your life's call is a journey in itself. In addition to associating with an accountability partner, commit to utilizing the legacy mapping theory (discussed herein in Chapter 4) to assist you on your journey to hearing and answering your own life's call. It is the kind of formation work that will challenge your thinking. When thinking is confronted seriously, the depth of clarity, change, and impact increase exponentially. Before turning to the legacy mapping theory, however, we will spend the next chapter examining the heart of leadership as defined in this work.

ILLUSTRATION 2.1

FORMATION IS THE RE-CONSTRUCTION OF YOU INTO THE PERSON YOU WERE INTENDED TO BE.

IMPORTANT TENETS OF FORMATION

Formation is foundational.

Positive change presupposes confronting
your growing edges.

Formation is a moral imperative
both in life and leadership.

Experiential formation teaches—
experience is life's greatest instructor.

Critical thinking and dialogue promote clarity
and growth at greater levels of depth.

The greatest leaders avoid shallow water thinking
in exchange for deep water mentality.

Extraordinary becomes possible
at the edge of comfort.

Surround yourself with those who think
at the level to which you aspire.

Values, character, integrity, morality,
and humanity are vital parts that make up
the inner person and are at the center
of experiential formation.

Formation is first intrapersonal
and second interpersonal.

Personal work is always an important
forerunner to public witness.

FIVE CRITICAL QUESTIONS TO ASSIST YOU IN THE FORMATION PROCESS

1. *Am I authentically connected to my source of power?*

2. *Am I daily accomplishing that which is meaningful and purposeful in connection with the person I intend to be?*

3. *Am I proceeding down the path that is set before me with clarity of vision?*

4. *Does my plan fully align with the mission to which my life is called?*

5. *Am I involved in transparent, accountable relationships that foster consistent self-reflection and intrapersonal development?*

Chapter 3

STARTING LINE CHALLENGE: RECOGNIZING AUTHENTIC LEADERSHIP

Having been variously defined in the many diverse venues in which it has become integrated, leadership is a well-worn term. From shore to shore and cradle to grave, we have become almost obsessed with the idea of leadership and as a result are regularly in search of "the one" who will turn out to be the next leader of this or that. With its increasing popularity, the term *leadership* has grown to mean many things to many people. This fact alone constrains me to commence this chapter on recognizing authentic leadership by sharing an image of what leadership means in this writing and perhaps in your life moving forward.

Simply expressed, leadership is the art of ethically influencing others to move toward a particular goal or specific achievement and is marked by intentionality and an attitude of service. The one who succeeds as a leader adds intention as an ingredient to his recipe for life. Moreover, leadership characterizes a journey, and a destination it is not. Unfortunately, but often, the person holding the title or position of leader is not necessarily regarded as such by others. This is so because the "true" leader is *always* the person who holds commanding influence regardless of the seat she occupies.

Furthermore, genuine leadership is evidenced not only by personal commitment but also moral commitment, and a great leader is determined to meld his moral responsibility to his person in order that he is led more by a desire to do good than personal gain. In reality, leadership esteems the other more than being about the "one" called leader. As such, authentic leadership is more about those whom you serve than those who serve you. Therefore, the greatest leaders are committed to and steadfast in the service of others. They have, in effect, learned the law of sowing and reaping—that is, one reaps what he sows. Those who sow sparingly are preparing to reap sparingly. Likewise, those who sow in abundance are preparing to reap abundance. In that way, the greatest leaders have come to appreciate the necessity in making the kind of contributions in the lives of others that cause them to define leadership rather than allowing leadership, as defined by the finite language of our vocabulary, to epitomize them.

The current time in which we live demands that leadership is expressed in ways different than in former times. The fact is carrying out leadership in a different manner is today's imperative, yet many leaders have not fully grasped this reality. I think of it like this: Leadership of yesterday was individual, directional, and in lawyers terms billable. What do I mean? I mean to suggest that leadership done the old way focused on the needs of the individual leader. The spotlight was on the leader and what he desired to accomplish rather than taking into consideration the value of the ideas of others.

It was directional because it was about having and exercising the power to direct someone or (better) tell someone else what to do. In other words, old forms of leadership are more about managing than leading. What is more, the style of management was top down rather than fluid, and very little autonomy was afforded to members of the team. As such, the potential for others to achieve beyond expectations was limited. Today's budding leaders are much more independent and fearless than in days of old. In that way, budding leaders are not afraid to strike out on their own and at a very early age. More importantly, the days of working for a company until someone in leadership takes note of what a talented, potential leader has to offer are long gone. That level of patience is a thing of the past.

Finally, the old style of leadership was billable. It was billable because much of the focus was on the amount of money the leader could or would amass as a result of his leadership. Many leaders seemed more concerned about the growth of their financial portfolio as over against how others (except the chosen few) might also be given an opportunity to build financial security. The Wall Street disaster and its negative impact on the global economy is a strong indicator of the old form of leadership.

Today, however, the world is calling for leadership to be accomplished in a different manner. In fact, true leadership demands it. Instead of being individual, directional, and billable, leadership is more impactful when it is relational, connectional, and sacrificial. Take a few moments to think about some of the leaders you most respect—especially those who have become world leaders and who have had the greatest positive impact on the lives of others. In all likelihood, their leadership is/was characterized by an ability to build amazing relationships, a commitment to foster deeply rooted connections with others, and a willingness to serve humanity. Incidentally, by connections I do not mean to suggest connections as in "network connections." Anyone can selfishly connect with others in order to further build individual success. Rather, I am suggesting true leadership requires not only that we be in relationship with others but also that we build strong, authentic, transparent, and impactful connections with others not merely for personal gain but for the good of the global community. In reality, being connected is the link that takes relationship to the next level. Relationship presupposes you are at least in the same room with others while connection advocates sharing space with others. More important, leadership that is relational, connectional, and sacrificial is typified by behaviors and character traits that are humanity-minded. And as one friend has reminded me, there can be "no legacy without humanity."[4] Correspondingly, now is a great time to contemplate your own leadership paralleled against relationship, connection, and sacrifice as characteristics that illustrate genuine leadership.

Like most things in life, leadership begins with a thought or idea, and in all likelihood the idea is that you as a person have some quality or characteristic that uniquely positions you to positively influence the behavior of others. To move the idea into action requires work on your part—especially if legacy is your targeted leadership finish line. Truly impactful leadership is characterized by progression, and it begins in the trenches of formation. The transformation process leads to an understanding of the importance of relationship. Relationship leads to a realization of the critical nature of genuine connections with others, and the truly connected leader understands the gift in giving and serving others at the level of sacrifice.

---

[4] Quote by Benee Brown, Pharm.D.

ILLUSTRATION 3.1

Relational Leadership

LEADERSHIP IS NOT ADVANCED BY THE NUMBER OF PEOPLE YOU ENCOUNTER; RATHER, ITS POWER IS IN THE DEPTH OF THE TRANSACTION!

Authentic Leadership Is Relational

Leadership that is relational emphasizes the importance of relationship as a core strength and necessity in working with others. Relational leaders recognize no person is an island, and we were designed to exist in community, which means we share ideas and make ourselves available and accountable on the road we travel with others. In fact, forging strong relationships and supporting the work of others is quintessential leadership. Moreover, leadership that is truly relational understands relationship to mean establishing ties and strong bonds with others. It necessitates intentionality and meaningful interactions and recognizes the value in others. Relational leadership abandons the notion of lack of concern for others, and it refrains from self-centered or self-serving attitudes and behavior. It respects mutuality and acknowledges the critical nature of interdependence. In that way, genuinely relational leadership means we are keenly aware of our need for an-other. Truthfully, as leaders we must learn to be at ease living in this manner.

As relational beings, we fully understand that we not only rely upon but also are dependent upon one another. In fact, I strongly contend we are meant to exist in relationship as over against isolation, especially as it pertains to leadership. Further, I argue relational leadership is or should be characterized by the virtue of trust. It calls for you as a leader to show yourself trustworthy so that others will develop trust in you. Trust is a solid foundation to enhance relationship and encourage a true expression of human interdependence and meaningful support between individuals.

Relational leadership is characterized by a desire to find commonality with others. It also understands while difference must be respected, as a human race individuals have far more in common than in difference. The gift is in recognizing the value and strength in both the difference and the commonalities. What is more, the greatest leaders seek out ways to put to use the diverse and common gifts of many. Relational leadership also comprehends the reciprocal nature of relationship and understands doing for others will prompt others in like manner. True relational leadership also prompts the virtue of doing unto others as you desire others would do unto you. Stated another way, true leaders live in such a fashion that they treat others in the same way in which they desire to be treated by others.

Relational leaders, who are both intentional and authentic in their dealings with others, do not concern themselves with whether or not forgiveness is merited; rather, they recognize giving and receiving unmerited forgiveness paves the way for transformation. True relational leadership suggests that you as a leader think before speaking and engaging in dialogue but at the same time create an environment that invites others to connect through open and honest communication—an ideology that pushes the envelope of relationship. It also necessitates operating from a place of respect for self and others and promotes discovering the joy in extending grace.

Relational leaders are reliable, and they speak and walk in truth. In fact, they give power to truth by speaking in the positive and declaring those transforming things that are not as though they were not just in their own lives but also in the lives of others. Moreover, they understand the power of life and death resides in the tongue, and they choose to speak life, understanding its inherent power. Those who practice relational leadership work to break negative cycles and are life-giving sources. They align their actions with their tongue and their tongues with their action. They are motivated to move with a "sign" of victory even when it appears they are being met with defeat, as they walk by faith and not by sight and recognize the importance of setting such an example before others.

Leaders who have truly embraced the importance of relationship are contemplative; they cast vision that motivates others beyond their places of comfort and utilize strategy to chart their course. They understand vision is the art of seeing the invisible and that faith is the substance of things hoped for and the evidence of things not yet seen. They are the kind of leaders who are neither afraid nor ashamed to say what they believe and live by what they say. They have learned the significance of spending their time on the offense rather than in a defensive posture, as they understand far more value is created for all in the positive space of the offense.

Leaders who clearly comprehend the value in relational

leadership understand the tremendous responsibility in dealing with self and others and say what they mean and mean what they say. Relational leaders live in a manner that leaves others better for having encountered them whether they meet one or many. They have come to appreciate leadership is not advanced by the number of people you encounter; rather, its power is in the depth of the transaction. They have defined their rules of the road in the form of a value system containing boundaries by which they live, function, operate, and interact with others. They have learned the idea of core values is neither unique nor exclusive to the corporate arena and have adopted their own core values that guide their leadership as well as their relationship with others. Here are some examples of core values to consider: (1) to live a life that honors morality, justice and integrity; (2) to live a relational life dedicated to service and respecting the value in others; (3) to build character from the inside out; (4) to walk in humility; and (5) to live in reflection carefully critiquing your actions against the person you profess to be.

With a solid value system in place, a relational leader can model the outcomes she desires to see in those who follow as well as those who peer as onlookers from the sidelines. In other words, the greatest leaders understand one cannot add value without first possessing value motivated by a firm internal value system. Stated another way, values lived is intrinsic to value added, and a leader ought to add value in the lives of others. Moreover, a leader's values speak volumes about the man or woman in the mirror, and authentic leaders understand they accomplish that in which they have placed value. Finally, relational leadership requires consistency (especially in dealing with others) except when remaining consistent would be inconsistent with the values and principles of leadership that foster personal values and service to others.

To put relational leadership to work in your life, consider the ways in which you can be receptive to the value in others, more supportive of those you are assigned to lead, more inclusive in strategy and planning, more generous in sharing knowledge and wisdom, more open to receiving ideas and input from others, more liberal in spreading responsibility, more respectful of difference, more appreciative of commonalities, less focused on self, more intentional in concern for others, and more willing to admit your success is directly tied to the success of others. In short, leadership contemplates relating to others. How well you learn to relate will directly correlate to how others perceive you as a leader.

Connectional Leadership

CONNECTIONAL LEADERSHIP COMES INTO REACH WHEN A LEADER DARES TO ASK HIMSELF THESE TOUGH QUESTIONS: WHO HAS NEED OF ME, AND WHERE AM I BEING SUMMONED TO GO?

Authentic Leadership Is Connectional

One of the greatest rewards in life is the gift of authentically connecting with others. To be truly connected with others, as a leader, requires a kind of interconnectedness that fully appreciates the reliance of the gift of one upon the gift of others—that is, my gift cannot be fully expressed absent my relationship with and to others. Think about it like this: Genuinely connected leadership nurtures the possibility that my interrelatedness to an-other allows us to inspire the best in one another. More importantly, connection is the antithesis of envy and strife. Thus, to reach the mark of authentic, connectional leadership necessitates realizing "team" and teamwork. In essence, it takes relationship to the next level.

As an example, I am reminded of my days of running track and being a part of the 440 relay team. To be a winning team required not only that we knew each other's skills and abilities but also that we each put forth our best effort in order that we might enhance the gifts of the other members of the team. In other words, I was clear that the best in me inspired the best in each of my teammates. Additionally, because we were functioning as a team we each had a deep desire to perform at our absolute best in order that we would succeed as a team. My success was directly tied to the success of each other member, and understanding such was a critical imperative to understanding connection. There could be no space for envy, strife, jealousy, or communication failures. There could be no winner and loser on the same team. If one of us won, that automatically meant we all won. Similarly, if one of us lost that also meant we all lost.

Further, I argue it is virtually impossible to achieve connectional leadership absent authenticity and transparency. I maintain that genuine connection with others is possible only when I walk in authenticity and become vulnerable with others. In addition, once I have learned what it really means to walk in my authentic self I must likewise become transparent in my dealings with others. (See Chapter 5 for a greater discussion of authenticity and transparency in leadership.)

For the moment, however, it is important to note authentically and transparently connecting with others involves the task of first knowing yourself. Moreover, the process of self-examination better prepares a leader for the task of connecting with others. In other words, a leader cannot share with others what he has not already achieved for himself. Thus, genuine, "connected" leadership is fostered through self-reflection and consistent self-examination followed by self-enrichment or intrapersonal development—that is, once I have grown as a leader, I am more capable of inspiring growth in others through strong interpersonal competence. Likewise, the connected leader is capable of understanding issues but more importantly is intimately familiar with the inherent value in understanding the person across the table. The key, though, is in understanding I must first know myself after which I am capable of understanding others.

Connected leaders understand the concept of "every

member, one body," signifying the many talents and gifts of the members of their team, yet they are called together to work as one. Parenthetically, leaders who are committed to the idea of connection recognize the value of humanity and "mine" the gifts in themselves and others for the common and greater good. Connected leaders are not motivated by the idea of amassing wealth and power; rather, they are encouraged by the number of lives they positively impact, as they refuse to measure success by net worth instead of self-worth. They fully understand the more value they add to the lives of others the greater the connection they are apt to build. Thus, truly connectional leadership comes into reach when a leader dares to ask himself these tough questions: Who has need of me, and where am I being summoned to go?

Additionally, a truly connected leader apprehends a responsibility to the lives of the one and the many. Consequently, he holds to that which he believes. As well, he believes in himself and in the power of humankind to give life to dreams, hopes, convictions, and realities that can change the course and direction of the lives of the downtrodden—connected at its best. Accordingly, he remembers to count his blessings not by material possessions but by the number of people in need he has helped. In that way, truly connected leaders are not apprehensive about empowering others to "walk" in their giftedness, and they understand the value in surrounding themselves with those who possess gifts different and often greater even than their own. They have "grown" to understand the true value in connectedness appreciates the power in linking gifts. Think of it like the leadership abilities displayed in Phil Jackson when he coached the Chicago Bulls to six NBA championships. He had the right talent in the right positions, and they understood the value in being connected as a team. The members of the team played their best and inspired each other to amazing results.

Connected leaders are conscious of the fact their achievements were stimulated by those who came before and whose sacrifice paved the way for their contributions to and in the lives of others. Hence, connected leaders recognize the great ones who have come before and view their contributions and lessons as gifts to help light the pathway for their own leadership journey.

Not surprisingly, truly connected leaders are powered by enormous inner strength, and they strive to help others find their voice. As such, I am reminded of my favorite movie of all time: *Mr. Holland's Opus*. Mr. Holland was a frustrated composer who spent thirty years as a high school music teacher who clearly understood the importance of harmony in giving voice to melody. At the same time, he was not aware of the true gift of leadership he had shown to all of his music students during his three decades of teaching. But upon retirement, his students from across so many years gathered to play the opus that he had been creating during his entire teaching career. And so it is with truly connected leaders; they find in others the gift of accord (connection), which ultimately creates a song.

ILLUSTRATION 3.3

Sacrificial Leadership

GREAT LEADERS BREAK THROUGH LIMITATIONS
AND SACRIFICE TO BREAK DOWN BARRIERS ACROSS
RACIAL, SOCIAL, CULTURAL, ETHNIC, ECONOMIC,
CLASS, AND EVEN RELIGIOUS LINES.

Authentic Leadership Is Sacrificial

You might recall my story in Chapter 1 about a friend who during the course of my writing asked me whether or not it is really possible to know if indeed one has led well. Of course, he is a lawyer friend, and we are known to find a question in what many would consider a fact. As I think about it more, in all honesty, I maintain the answer begins at the place of sacrifice. Accordingly, the question you as a leader might ask yourself is this: What shall I pursue? The answer I contend might reveal the importance of pursuing what is good, ethical, just, and moral. In short, what good will you do (or are you doing) for the sake of enriching someone else? Have your life experiences reiterated leadership is not about the leader? Have you learned leadership is all about the *other*, and genuine leaders are not afraid to check their armor (accomplishments) at the door in order to enter with the mind of a servant?

The fact is sacrificial leadership is conspicuous by its authenticity, transparency, ethical conduct, global mind-set (my reach is longer than I think), communal commitment, and social consciousness. In short, it is "real" and servant based. Moreover, leaders who have grasped the concept of sacrifice are not involved to build a name, and they realize an investment in others is an investment in themselves and society at large. Leaders whose mission is service give voice to those who have no voice and dignity to those who society says require no dignity, as they fully comprehend the value in *all* humanity. They appreciate the diverse nature of the world in which we live, and they celebrate difference as a symbol of God's divine power to create a communal human race as opposed to separate and unequal ethnic races. In that way, sacrificial leaders willingly break through limitations and work to break down barriers across racial, social, cultural, ethnic, economic, class, and even religious lines. In fact, they realize an authentic leader is also an advocate, and advocacy—as I see it—is understanding and acting upon the power of possibility.

The leader who has truly embraced service to others as his underlying purpose is not distracted by what is not and understands he must get out of the boat in order to walk on water and move from the side of the road in order to build a bridge. In other words, the strength of his contribution to others is in the sacrifice he is willing to make on behalf of an-other—that is, the one who is truly ready for sacrifice is willing to offer deeds that benefit others and is purposed to conduct his affairs ethically and with integrity. More importantly, he is guided by that which is just.

So you ask what is at the core of this idea of sacrificial leadership? Leadership that is based upon a model of sacrifice contemplates my willingness to forego some right or privilege for the betterment of others, and it forces me to understand betterment is not defined according to my selfish wants. Rather, it is defined by enrichment to others. Thus, the sacrificial leader comprehends fully the advantage to which he has been given access and is prepared to set aside some personal privilege for someone else's greater gain. It places the needs of others squarely within my path, and it challenges me as a leader to consider whether or not my belief system around leadership requires redefinition. It encourages me toward the superior value of giving as over against receiving while simultaneously teaching me that giving paves the way for me to receive at much greater levels than can be achieved when I stand only in a place expecting to receive.

Sacrificial leadership induces me to operate out of the virtue of love inspiring outreach at significantly greater levels. It causes me to think about whether or not I am really my brother's keeper. It prompts me to look at the various ways in which I can sow positively into the lives of others—especially those in need. It offers me the honor of taking up a stake in an impactful cause and of making the necessary sacrifices to create a difference. It inspires me toward challenging systems that foster inferiority and oppress others. It means I willingly surrender something of value in my own life in order to make better the life of someone else. It pushes me toward a true understanding that life and leadership are no longer all about me and prompts my availability at life-giving levels inspiring life-changing results that uplift others. It takes relational and connectional to the next level as the final progression in moving from a philosophy of me to an ideology of us. In that way, it redefines me as a leader.

Doctors who serve in underdeveloped countries or in

underprivileged communities when they could serve elsewhere and make considerably more money doing so provide a great example. Likewise, lawyers who make sacrifices to take up causes such as criminal justice reform or who sacrifice time and the potential for making a great deal more money donating legal services or providing such at substantially reduced rates are another example. The tens of thousands of men and women who serve their countries in times of war and peace are also examples.

One other thought provoking example comes to mind. One morning while engaged in my daily discipline of walking I witnessed a rather heated exchange between a construction worker and an apparently frustrated driver who was attempting to make a turn at an intersection that had been blocked for resurfacing. The scene was full of trucks, workers, equipment, other drivers, and pedestrians. (It was ripe for an accident.) Here is what I saw: A medium-sized male construction worker stepped in front of a vehicle and informed the driver he could not turn. A much larger and very angry male driver emerged from a small black truck and informed the construction person he intended to turn. Although the driver was visibly very upset and yelling very loudly, the worker stood his ground. From the sidewalk I could hear him say, "My job is to protect this intersection and keep my co-workers from getting hit, and you will *not* endanger them by turning at this intersection." Although the driver yelled even louder about what he was going to do and got back into his truck and revved his engine (as if preparing to "run over" someone), the worker still stood his ground. In fact, I also heard the worker say, "You will just have to hit me because I am not moving. I am not allowing you to put their lives in jeopardy. You must keep straight." A now extremely angry driver revved his engine again and pulled away while running over cones and almost hitting another construction worker who was holding the construction stop sign.

At first, the exchange I witnessed appeared to be two angry men standing their ground. On second blush, however, the leadership lesson became apparent. The construction worker not only took his position seriously but also was prepared to make a sacrifice on behalf of those with whom he worked. He understood his position was not all about him and that he was required to proceed on behalf of others. Whether or not the worker took seriously the threats of the driver or the driver was serious is not my real focus here, as I clearly believe the driver was angry and bluffing. He wanted his way but learned a few threats were insufficient to deter a determined leader. Rather, the lesson from this example stems from the manner in which the construction worker approached his leadership responsibility. He took the idea of sacrifice seriously.

The Next Step:
Making it a Generation to Generation Imperative

Finally, I assert that since the most impactful leadership is relational, connectional, and sacrificial it must also be intergenerational. Leadership is intergenerational in that it is incumbent upon those who understand authentic leadership to appreciate the critical nature in helping the generations that follow to recognize and value what genuine leadership is and is not. As leaders of today, it is important to pass leadership values and essentials to the leaders of tomorrow. It is also vital to understand that future generations learn not from what is said but more from what is achieved and the examples that are lived. Those lessons begin as close as your home and spread accordingly. That kind of leadership is a trigger causing other leaders to understand the truth—"the more we give, the more we will receive." The fact is it is leadership at an entirely different level. As a leader, are you taking the idea of sacrifice seriously? What will you sacrifice for the benefit of an-other? And what legacy will you leave to those who follow?

CRITICAL ASPECTS OF LEADERSHIP

— Leadership is relational, inviting true relationship with others.

— Leadership is connectional, necessitating real connection with others.

— Leadership is sacrificial, expecting an exchange— a giving up for someone else's gain.

— Leadership is intergenerational, begging to be shared with generations to come.

II

NAVIGATING
THE RACE

Chapter 4

THE LEGACY MAPPING THEORY

Now that you understand the importance of formation as foundation and recognize leadership as
relational, connectional, sacrificial, and intergenerational,
it is time to turn to the process of legacy mapping. Legacy
mapping is an essential aspect of formation. Formation, as
you learned in Chapter 2, is the reconstruction of you into
the person you were intended to be. Legacy mapping is the
process by which you begin your critical formation work.
Perhaps you are asking yourself these questions: What is
legacy mapping, and why should it matter in my life? These
are great questions and, in fact, ones I have previously asked
myself. Think of this book as your opportunity to tackle
these important questions head-on.

When I think of or engage the idea of legacy mapping, I
am referring to a critical, self-evaluative process designed to

assist a person in identifying his or her true vocation or call and the pathway to achieving personal purpose. Why would I term this process *legacy mapping*? It's simple: If you plan to create and leave an inheritance for others, it will require intentionality. It will require a road map. Intentionality implies planning and preparation. There is no substitute for preparedness, and in life you obtain that for which you have planned and prepared. Just like a monetary inheritance a parent intends to leave for a child requires intentionality around saving and investing, so it is with legacy mapping. While you were born for a purpose, purpose can only be achieved when you put in the time by specifically identifying that purpose, preparing for and planning the execution of that purpose, and taking the necessary action steps to carry out the plan you have developed. Incidentally, while there may be some who have stumbled into their life's work, legacy is far more likely when intentionality and specificity meet power and are intermingled with your formula for living and achieving. In short, legacy mapping is formation in process and preparation for legacy. Moreover, legacy is not a destination but a journey.

More important, since legacy denotes inheritance (and this book promotes legacy leadership), it necessarily follows as stated in Chapter 3 that leadership is intergenerational— a critical lesson for *all* leaders. Intergenerational simply implies that it relates to persons in different generations or age categories. All too often as leaders we have neglected to pass the greatest aspects and lessons of leadership to future generations. Consequently, whether you are a biological parent, surrogate parent, stepparent, adoptive parent, God parent, or even mentor, part of the responsibility of leading well is to pass leadership lessons and principles of leadership to the generations that follow. The values and principles discussed in this book are ideal candidates to begin the process of training future generations.

Imagine teaching your biological or surrogate offspring (mentees) or even those younger generations who work under your tutelage about the concept of formation and the tenets of integrity. Envision if they learned long before adulthood what it really means to listen for their life's call. Think of what it would mean if they learned early in life the ideals of relational, connectional, and sacrificial as the true components of leadership. Suppose they learned from their household of origin the importance in respecting difference and embracing commonality with others. Even greater, consider the difference it would make if you actually lived such a life before them. They would learn while simultaneously beginning the process of receiving a great inheritance—even before your life has concluded. That, indeed, would qualify as legacy.

The power in teaching future generations reminds me once again of my days of running track and being a part of the 440 relay team. Each person ran her very best in her leg of the race. Her goals were twofold: (1) to successfully pass the baton to the next person and (2) to maintain or capture the lead position in order to provide an advantage to her teammate for her leg of the race. This is precisely the reason parents and others choose to bequeath an inheritance to their descendants—to provide them with an advantage or head start in the race of life. As pertains to leadership, we owe as much to future generations. And it is not just a matter of what we tell them; it is more a matter of what we teach them by the ways in which we choose to live as leaders.

When I was growing up, my father taught me the importance of understanding directions and proficiency at map reading. In fact, he took the time to teach all of my siblings how to properly read a map. He often explained I would be able to go anywhere I wanted if only I could simply understand how to read a map. I took him seriously and have always embraced the idea of mapping out my road trips. I maintain this concept is equally impactful when applied to discovering and living out your true call in life.

Among other concepts (revealed herein), the legacy mapping theory teaches that you must stop talking and begin the process of being (who you are called to be), doing (what you are called to do), and achieving (what you are destined to achieve). If indeed you are preparing for legacy, remember with each promotion, whether personal or professional, your leadership challenge will grow. The test for many leaders is often related to a lack of preparation for the next level. Those who attain or have attained the highest levels of leadership in the corporate world understand this principle and more than likely have been mentored by the best; meticulously groomed for every promotion; and have participated in succession planning, image building, and some form of personal branding, not to mention having first cultivated their craft. Be assured as a leader you cannot successfully navigate the challenges of the next level where there is lack of preparation. The question for you to contemplate in your leadership journey then is what are you doing that prepares you for the next level. For some this might mean becoming more effective in your current role. For others it might suggest learning the difference between managing and leading. For others perhaps your test relates to spending more time with those who have enough nerve to challenge you to take your "game" to the next level.

As you re-examine your leadership dash, you must also ask yourself two additional important questions: What impact do I desire to achieve? Do I have a strategic plan for my journey? Attaining impact as a leader is no easy feat. All too often leaders stumble into positions without truly understanding if indeed they are walking and operating in the space for which they have been uniquely designed. As a leader, it is critically important for you to understand and embrace the work to which you have been specifically called. That means you must understand the critical nature of aligning your desire to achieve with the purpose to which your life is calling. To do so allows for much greater access to impact and therefore legacy as will be discussed later.

Truthfully, only a portion of your journey is completed by knowing what you desire to achieve and the specific purpose to which your life has been called. It is still critical to develop a strategic plan to carry out your purpose. To that end, use these five questions, previously identified at the conclusion of Chapter 2, to help guide your formation as you apply the legacy mapping theory to your own journey: (1) Am I authentically connected to my source of power? (2) Am I daily accomplishing that which is meaningful and purposeful in connection with the person I intend to be? (3) Am I proceeding down a path with clarity of vision for that which is set uniquely before me? (4) Does my plan fully align with the mission to which my life is being called? (5) Am I involved in transparent, accountable relationships that foster consistent and meaningful self-reflection and intrapersonal development?

THE POWER TRIAD

The Power Triad

The legacy mapping theory is illustrated in a practical tool called the Power Triad. The Power Triad is in essence your legacy map and serves to help you align your life with your leadership call. While the same components are used by each person who engages the concept of legacy mapping, the specifics of each component are unique to the person whose triad it is. It is called the Power Triad because it illustrates how your life's call will serve as the source of your power and in essence the central nervous system for your development into legacy leadership. The term triad is used not simply because it contains three sections but because of the meaning of the word triad. Did you know the word triad means harmony? Thus, it is critical that each element of the map have harmony with the rest. Moreover, the triad is made up of key legacy components, and the sum of its parts make up the whole reflective of a leader who has put all aspects of the triad—power, purpose, path, and plan—to work in his life. See the graph and explanation on the following pages to better understand how you can bring the Power Triad and legacy mapping to life in your own developmental process.

ILLUSTRATION 4.1

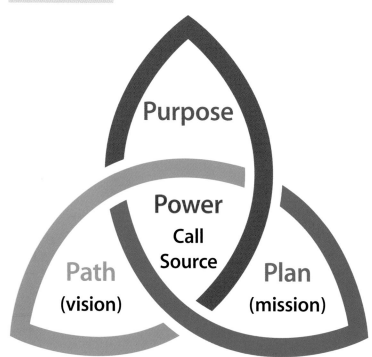

The Power Triad

LOOK CLOSELY AT THE DIAGRAM WHILE REVIEWING THE FOLLOWING SECTIONS TO HELP YOU UNPACK AND APPLY THE LEGACY MAPPING THEORY TO YOUR OWN LIFE AS LEADER.

Power

Many leaders have spent much of their leadership life in careers where they are good but admittedly are not in their true vocation. In fact, you probably know people like this or perhaps this is a description of you, and now you desire to find that true vocation to which you have been called. What happened? How did I end up here? These are often the questions one is left to ponder as they are looking retrospectively at their career. The truth is leaders often spend untold amounts of time chasing after what they think or have been told by others is their purpose. Many times the rationale for what leaders pursue is based solely upon skill or talent in a particular area. While skill is critical for success, skill alone does not answer the question related to "call" or source of power as termed in this writing. When a leader spends the bulk of his time chasing purpose, he sets himself up to neglect key opportunities to hear life's call. I think of it something like this: We pursue purpose, but the call pursues us. More important, when we are open to being pursued by the call, our purpose will be clarified. Remember, the call for your life can be drowned out if you are not in a place to hear it when it comes. Just like with the telephone where you live, you must be in a place to receive the call when the phone rings.

Consider this: The disconnect stems from the fact leaders all too often narrowly associate the word call only with ministry or one who holds a religious office. But as leaders each of us is being called, or "summoned," to some particular accomplishment. The source of power is contained within the call, and great leaders are not satisfied until they have discovered their call, or true vocation. I have come to understand it like this. You must first ask this question: What am I being called to do or accomplish? In turn, you must listen for your life's call. It is necessary because it positions you for the work that is yours to complete and is the place from which your power emanates. In other words, the call holds your power because the call represents your source, and source is defined as the place of origin. Power is the center force and is thus connected to each of the other components of the Power Triad. Consider how powerful it would be to live, work, and function from your place of origin—the place from which you were designed to lead also known as your place of power. What is more, what you are capable of accomplishing is so because of a greater source that has empowered you to achieve your purpose. For me, that source is God. Everything and every possibility emanates from my source. You may consider your source different than mine; however, the key is to know and connect authentically with your source.

Notice in the diagram that power is designated in red.

Red is used because of its strong symbolism. It is a color typically associated with passion, strength, bravery, and—for me—courage; all these qualities are critical to strong leadership. As an example of a call, one could be called to be a *leader's leader*. The call, in essence, identifies the big picture, and each step beyond the call gives greater clarity to the particular ways in which you have been summoned to fulfill the call.

Purpose

Once you have heard and identified your call, the next step includes pinpointing more specifically your purpose within the call. Purpose represents destination. Indeed, if you are called, then you are called for a reason and you are called to a destiny uniquely designed for you, and the process of reaching that place is a journey. An example of a purpose statement is *to advance the cause of justice by serving as an agent of change.* As you can see, the purpose statement is more specific than the call, as the call represents the bigger picture. The purpose statement, on the other hand, begins the process of giving specificity or greater clarity to how the call will be executed. As previously noted in Chapter 2, clarity is an absolute essential on the journey to fulfill your life's call. Without clarity, the opportunity for walking outside of purpose is greater. As a result, it is incumbent upon you as a leader to seek out clarity in reference to your life's work. Clarity is not a given and must be pursued as an important component of achieving your leadership destiny. In short, your prospects for accomplishing legacy are inextricably tied to clarity.

Moreover, it is critical to understand purpose is an outgrowth of power. In other words, your life's purpose is at the center of the call, which serves as the power source for your ultimate outcomes. The greatest leaders seek after their life's purpose and live by a vision and mission that emanate from the purpose to which they have been called. Their seeking is grounded in listening attentively for the call in their own lives, not the box someone else created and in which they are expected to live and lead.

Notice in the diagram purpose has been identified in the color purple. The color **purple** has traditionally been said to symbolize royalty, power, and authority. As a leader, you are being challenged to see yourself in the place to which you know you are called to contribute. Be assured that it is larger than you. If you discover the purpose to which you have been called is not larger than you, I suggest you have set your sights far below legacy and have not grasped the concept there is a force outside of you that is greater than you and that will lead you to achieve far more than you thought you could and certainly more than you could ever achieve on your own. Accomplishing at such a level, however, will require you to move outside your comfort zone. In fact, the possibility for achieving extraordinary begins at the edge of comfort. As long as you remain in comfort, you prevent something larger than you from transpiring. The force that is greater than you awaits your willingness to recognize that your limitations impede the force from moving your achievements from ordinary to extraordinary. The force is not needed to accomplish that which is already within your purview. The force is necessary to carry out that which exceeds your boundaries of ability.

Have you ever met someone who consistently appears to achieve the miraculous? How about someone who always has more support for his ideas than appears necessary? I contend that person has stretched himself beyond comfort and has set forth vision that inspires others to join his work. With that kind of support, one is destined to achieve far greater than he could achieve on his own. My best example of such is when a person undertakes the enormous task of campaigning for the office of president. He or she must certainly move outside of comfort and set forth a clear and concise vision that motivates others not only to join in the campaign but also to cast a ballot.

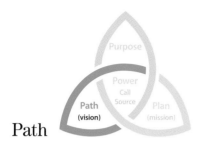

Path

The next step involves understanding the path. Path is equivalent to vision and is the beginning step of a leader charting the specific course for his journey. The path can be quantified in a vision statement for your life. An example of a vision statement is *to serve the needs of others through teaching, leading, training, and giving back.* Note how the path sets forth with even greater clarity the means by which the call is to be fulfilled.

Notice that the color used to identify the path in the diagram is green. The color **green** has typically symbolized nature, youth, and beginning (as in spring). For me, the color green symbolizes the pathway. Each of us has a particular path to travel in order to accomplish that which has been set before us. My path is unique to me, just as your path is unique to you. The use of green here also reminds me of the days of running track. Coach made it clear we had no chance of winning if we did not stay in our lane. The path, or pathway, is your lane, and it is calling you to finish the race that is set before you and you alone.

It is most important that you follow your designated path as over against attempting to follow the pathway that has been selected for someone else. Understanding your specific path is a call to authenticity and intentionality— that is, you must be intentional about walking authentically down the pathway for your life. The key is listening for the "prompts of life." You must listen for the road on which life is prompting you to travel. You must block out distractions as well as those who would discourage you from following the direction you are feeling from the deepest places of your innermost being. In order to hear the prompts of life, you must be in tune with self. You must have an idea about who you are and what drives you. You must make up in your mind that you will go even if you have to go alone.

Unfortunately, some leaders have missed their true mark because they allowed their focus to be diverted to the path that was intended for someone else. Think of the extraordinary gift the world receives when we each walk authentically down the path that is set before us. Then think how much greater the gift is when we allow our paths to work alongside others creating harmony and building success through unique gifts and commonalities alike.

Plan

Finally, there is the plan. The plan is your mission. It consists of the day-to-day workings for carrying out your purpose and vision, which ultimately relate back to the call. An example of a plan, or mission statement, is *to inspire others toward "just" living through principles of transformational leadership.* So, in this Power Triad example, the leader's daily work is in the area of transformational leadership.

Notice the color used to identify the plan in the diagram is blue. Here the color **blue** symbolizes direction or the blueprint. In architecture, the most well constructed homes meet the specifications set forth in the blueprint.[5] This is so because in developing the blueprint the architect has considered what structural layout will produce the strongest building that will withstand the elements of weather and time. The same is true in a life dedicated to fulfilling purpose. It requires a well-developed, written plan. In fact, not much that is extraordinary will be accomplished without a life blueprint. In short, this plan will serve as your guide for carrying out the daily workings of the vocation to which

---

[5]In architecture, the blueprint is actually captured in blue.

you are called. A well-executed plan opens the gateway for achieving success. The path and the plan are the tactical pieces and, therefore, are resources that help you make progress along the journey. The resources are there to keep you focused on your vision and mission and translate them into specific and measurable deliverables for the ultimate completion of the call for your life.

Think of it like this: The call is bigger than you and makes it possible for ordinary people to achieve the extraordinary. The call, in essence, holds the power and is, therefore, your source. Purpose is connected to and emanates from the power and is closely tied to the source. They are, in effect, the strategic elements of the Power Triad. It is important to understand the difference between the source and resources of the Power Triad. Often in life we begin to focus on resources neglecting to stay connected and focused on the source. The source is our power and will give us the ability to properly utilize our resources to achieve legacy. You must decide for yourself to take this process seriously. Set your sights on receiving and hearing the call, naming your purpose, outlining your path, and setting the plan in place followed by a walk down the road of integrity. Before taking up the next section of the book, set aside some time to consider your formation journey and begin charting out what the Power Triad would look like if applied specifically to your legacy map.

IMPORTANT LEGACY TAKEAWAYS

— Legacy mapping is a critical, self-evaluative process designed to assist a person in identifying his or her true vocation or call and the pathway to achieving personal purpose.

— The Power Triad is the practical legacy mapping tool, which serves to align your life with your leadership call.

— The source of power is contained within the call, and great leaders are not satisfied until they have discovered their call or true vocation.

— Your life's purpose is at the center of the call, which serves as the power source for your ultimate outcomes.

— Your path is the equivalent to a vision for your life and is the beginning step of a leader charting the specific course for his life's journey.

— The plan is your mission and consists of the day-to-day workings for carrying out your purpose and vision, which ultimately relate back to your life's call.

*"We pursue purpose,
but the call pursues us."*

— Geneace Williams

Chapter 5

CHARTING YOUR PATHWAY TO GREAT LEADERSHIP

Now that we have tackled the legacy mapping theory and its application tool (the Power Triad), I have news for you. It is not enough to simply embrace the Power Triad unless, of course, your greatest desire is to attain the title of leader. If that is the case, perhaps it is not necessary for you to read the remainder of this book. If, on the other hand, your desire is toward creating legacy in leadership, read on because hearing the call, identifying your purpose, charting your path, and developing a plan are not enough. The Power Triad is critical but not sufficient on its own. A destiny-bound journey requires a model by which one lives and carries out the purpose to which he or she has been called. In essence, the Power Triad helps you recognize and identify your leadership map. Thereafter, there is the detail of how one fully lives into purpose or legacy—the important mile markers for your journey, if you will.

To help you with your leadership dash, I have identified important mile markers and developed them into a model that I have termed the *Integrity-Based Leadership Model (IBLM)*. The mile markers are more about how you live as a leader, which ultimately paves the way for what you are able to accomplish. The model contains five distinct leadership principles and is designed to help leaders chart the course to their greatest leadership contribution. In the paragraphs that follow, I will discuss the relevance, importance, and specific elements and deliverables contained in each principle. These "living" principles are crucial elements on the road to creating legacy in leadership.

*FIVE "LIVING" ESSENTIALS ON THE
PATHWAY TO LEGACY LEADERSHIP*

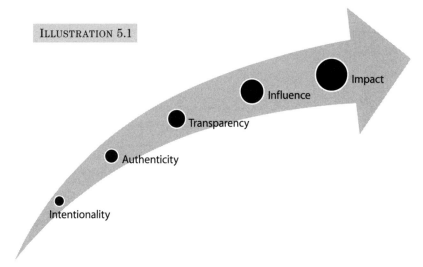

ILLUSTRATION 5.1

INTEGRITY-BASED LEADERSHIP MODEL
YIELD = IMPACT
IMPACT = LEGACY

I am sure most readers would not set out on a journey to an unfamiliar place without first gathering the pertinent mapping information or certainly at a minimum the street address. Likewise, genuine leaders would not embark upon their leadership journey without engaging in legacy mapping. Having been introduced to the legacy mapping theory, you are now challenged to consider how you will integrate the IBLM into your leadership journey. The IBLM is a values-based model consisting of five core value-based leadership principles that are important elements for any leader to have as a part of his leadership tool kit.

Indeed, the greatest leaders fully understand that leading from a place of the highest integrity is a liberating journey, a continuum, a process that starts small and ends large. Its impact is life changing for the leader as well as those who are positively influenced by who the leader really is. True integrity is human witness, and there can be no legacy without human witness. Human witness relates to our understanding of the importance of human dignity. Human dignity points to the needs of others and shouts leadership from a place of service. We are our brother's keeper!

One of the greatest examples of human witness I have recently seen exemplified is in the title used by Pastor Frank Anthony Thomas. Thomas refers to himself as the Senior Servant of Mississippi Boulevard Christian Church. The use of this title strongly suggests he understands his role as leader to be that of servant. Moreover, by using this title I would argue he understands that human witness is inherent in service to others. Parenthetically, it is essential to note it is not sufficient for a leader to simply utilize a title that denotes service to others. It must be lived out in how the leader conducts his daily affairs in his role as leader. It is also important to note service in leadership is not confined to religious leaders. Rather, serving others is a critical imperative in leadership regardless of the area in which you lead.

The principles that create the pathway to legacy leadership and make up the IBLM are termed "living," as they must come alive and be lived out in every facet of your existence. From business dealings to personal relationships, from matters of the head to matters of the heart, the pathway to genuine leadership is paved by fully embracing and living out these principles. In that way, you work to align personal goals with professional goals and vice versa. To be successful, you must approach the journey with intention and purpose. You must intend to walk in integrity and purpose in your heart nothing will stand between you and your goal, understanding integrity also means avoiding the very appearance of evil or impropriety.

The concept of leading with integrity contemplates the utmost in moral character and an uncompromising commitment to moral and ethical conduct. It means as a leader you follow the highest code of ethics and refuse to wait for others to pen your ethical mode of operation. Rather, you set your own code of ethics by the highest standards and by living into the principles of the IBLM. Because of the collapse of our economy, in this day and time, integrity is being examined with much greater scrutiny. As a result, the greatest leaders will appreciate all the more the value in a moral and ethical compass and will willingly and continuously strive toward that end. Further, integrity is intricately intertwined with each of the five principles that work in concert to bring the model to life. To be complete, integrity must not only be intentional but also authentic and transparent. You must live it, confess you live it, and show others you live it, as one cannot achieve authenticity outside of integrity. The truth is inauthenticity is the antithesis of integrity. Thus, it is critical for a leader to walk in authenticity. When you show up, others should be able to discern the real you is in the room. In addition, transparency cannot be attained without both authenticity and integrity, and integrity is paramount to fully and positively influence and impact the lives of others.

Finally, it is critical to know the pathway to legacy leadership is not simply about a new way of living. It is not possible to achieve a complete new way of living without also adopting a new way of thinking. So daily you must seriously contemplate whether you are living with intention, walking in authenticity, offering the transparent you, ethically and morally influencing others for the greater good, and creating impact that presupposes legacy. The journey to uncompromising integrity is just that. It is a journey that requires consistent self-examination and continual effort on the road to living fully into integrity. You must think about where you are on the continuum. You must think about what integrity means to you as well as what integrity really means and be willing to align your thinking and behavior with the highest level of integrity. You must be willing to do the right thing even when others are going in the opposite direction. You will know you are moving in the right direction when what you contemplate meets moral, ethical, and legal barometers.

Intentionality

> *Leadership that reaches legacy is intentional, not accidental.*

The greatest leaders pursue leadership roles understanding leadership is part of their DNA. In other words, genuine leaders embrace leadership with full knowledge leadership is a call to be lived in and through their purpose. That which is done with intention is done with purpose, and when purpose is the driving factor for a particular action, it results in a more meaningful outcome. Stated another way, when intention meets purpose it sets the stage for transformation, and authentic leadership is born from life's transformational moments. The best leaders also embrace the fact that they may not have been born leaders but recognize they were born to lead. In this way, true leaders, like great athletes, great actors, or great writers, work at fully developing their craft. More important, leaders are not only intentional about their quest for leadership but also about other aspects of their lives. For example, they are intentional about relationships and those with whom they keep company, as they understand fully leadership is relational. In fact, they understand leadership does not exist outside of relationship. With such an understanding, it becomes easier for leaders to be intentional about making a difference in someone else's life.

Genuine leaders are also intentional about the pursuit of their life's vision, being their best, giving their all, and finishing well. They are intentional about self-knowledge, self-care, and self-development. They have learned one's own self-development helps them live intentionally and more authentically in relation to others. True leaders understand that to reach their anticipated goal they must wake up each day with new intention and new drive to be better, to do better, to live better, to love better, to forgive better, and to become better. They recognize the critical imperative of self-reflection is even more important than pointing out the growing edges that exist in others.

Personal branding is one area of leadership development that is closely tied to intentionality. Corporate entities have long understood the concept of branding and its role in establishing loyalty. Corporations appreciate the connection between brand, brand value, and brand loyalty. In more recent times, however, the concept of branding has been discussed and promoted in relation to individuals. The idea is to build value by creating a personal brand. A brand is an identifier that is unique. It links a product to a trademark, and organizations go to great lengths to protect their brand. There are certain brand names like Mercedes-Benz or BMW that are immediately recognizable when mentioned. In that context, brand can be defined as something which is known, possessing an identity that is distinguishable and that offers or makes a commitment, which is genuinely backed by the power of the brand's influence. Brand is part thinking or attitude and part strategy; it is who you are and for what you stand. In personal branding, attitude reflects your inner personal development. At the same time, in this context strategy is more a tactical device because it contemplates the translation of attitude into a plan that when executed results in effective branding. It results in others knowing who you are and for what you stand.

The term *personal branding* is thought to have originated in a 1997 article authored by Tom Peters and published in *Fast Company* magazine. In his article, entitled "The Brand Called You," Peters wrote the following:

What Makes You Different?

Start right now: as of this moment you're going to think of yourself differently! You're not an "employee" of General Motors, you're not a "staffer" at General Mills, you're not a "worker" at General Electric or a "human resource" at General Dynamics (oops, it's gone!). Forget the Generals! You don't "belong to" any company for life, and your chief affiliation isn't to any particular "function." You're not defined by your job title and you're not confined by your job description. Starting today you are a brand.[6]

---

[6] Tom Peters, "The Brand Called You," Fast Company, August 1997, 10.

The concept of personal branding is still growing today, thirteen years after Mr. Peters first introduced the idea. In essence, the personal branding process contemplates an individual's development in the areas of skill, knowledge, and social and professional networking to personal appearance (including clothing) and personal presentation. A person's brand is embodied in his/her attitude, and a brand must be strategically positioned to capture the attention of others. Many leaders, however, have not achieved success in building a personal brand because their time has been spent embodying the brands of the companies for which they work. Yet the best leaders have come to understand the necessity of creating "personal brand" even in instances where they are employed by companies with a brand they wish to promote. The goal is to enhance the person as a complete package with a distinctive identity. The result is creation of a valuable asset leading to greater opportunities for personal and professional advancement. After engaging in the process of personal branding, a leader should be recognizable to others by the quality and character she exhibits. The secret is that even in instances where the leader is employed by a company (other than his or her own) the personal branding process will enhance how that leader presents on behalf of the company for which he works (and in turn himself). As a result, potential customers may be more likely to transact business with the company. All in all, it makes for a win-win situation.

It is important to note that care must be applied in personal branding for the simple fact I do not mean to suggest putting on a false or created self for the purpose of capturing the attention of others. Rather, I mean to suggest personal branding is an individual, developmental process that helps a leader cultivate an image and persona that is unique, authentic, and value added.

While personal branding is considered a more recent concept, there are clear historical examples of those who were quite successful in building a personal brand. As one example, the story of the life of Jesus Christ is arguably the first instance of true personal branding. There are certain characteristics and character traits in the story of His life that point to His very unique and distinguishable personhood. His love for His enemies, forgiveness of His assassins, His affinity for the oppressed and downtrodden, and His willingness to lay down His life for friends are just a few illustrations of His very unique assets. His accomplishments on earth led to His "brand" as Savior and created enduring value for those who believe. His story symbolizes legacy. In fact, His story gave life to legacy. Interestingly, historical accounts of the life of Jesus also suggest He lived a very intentional life, as He stayed focused on His mission during His life on earth—that is, He remained centered on His reason for living. He was careful not to allow others to influence Him down a path that was contrary to what He believed about His life's call. I would argue that whether one is a believer or not the account of His life indicates His intentionality around the work to which He was called.

Take some time to think about historical figures that

may have influenced your leadership journey. I, for instance, was very influenced by Dr. Martin Luther King Jr., whose love ethic persuaded me and was unmistakably a hallmark of his leadership. Furthermore, he was unquestionably intentional about his life's work, which was dedicated to building a beloved community of justice, faith, and hope. In fact, I argue his intentionality around his life's work made a distinguishable difference in his personal brand and ultimate global contributions.

That said, I contend it is important to understand true personal branding cannot be achieved outside of intentionality as well as authenticity. Even in the process of building a personal brand, it is a necessity for one to understand himself and to value his uniqueness and authenticity to the point of developing the brand that is unique to him. Personal branding is not being a carbon copy of everything or everyone else. It is about improving the authentic self that is your own. One area that may be overlooked by many endeavoring to establish a personal brand has to do with the development of the inward man or inward woman. I maintain one cannot develop a successful and appealing personal brand without taking some of the focus off of outward appearance and altering it such that he is intentional about the person he is from the inside out.

Inside-out transformation requires understanding and embracing the idea and concept of letting go. One of the things I have learned as a leader is that leaders often do a terrific job at taking on and embracing new challenges and new responsibilities. Leaders seem always prepared to take on the new challenge associated with growing their leadership footprint. On the contrary, leaders may not be as successful at mastering the art of letting go. Letting go of the past and past things that have occurred in life are far more difficult than simply taking on a new challenge and piling on more. The challenge to you as a leader is to understand what and when to let go, which might require receiving or extending unmerited forgiveness. Forgiveness is a powerful "weapon," and unmerited forgiveness is one example of letting go. In fact, I would argue forgiveness raises your leadership capital. It lends significant meaning to the concept: Never give your enemy what he deserves. Likewise, it understands the critical nature of extending forgiveness to others. No doubt, as you sit reading this book you stand in need of someone's forgiveness. Forgiveness allows release, and it liberates the soul. When you open your hands and release, you open up yourself to receive that which awaits you.

Authenticity

> *Authenticity requires self-awareness, self-development, and self-discipline.*

Authentic leadership is genuine or real, and authentic leaders conduct themselves and their affairs/business in a "what you see is what you get" manner. Authenticity compels a level of genuineness beyond the surface, and authentic leaders are willing to ask hard questions of themselves and others. At the same time, authentic leaders face themselves before considering a face-off with others. They choose depth over facade and truth over deceit. Even more transforming, authenticity allows leaders to first set and exceed honest, forthright, personal expectations and then gives them permission to urge others toward the same level of courage and self-discipline. The fact is authentic leaders will not ask of others what they will not first do themselves.

Authentic leaders are busy about discovering their true person and "stirring up the gift" that is within them. They desire to walk in purpose and develop into the unique persons they were intended to be, understanding to live any other way is to live beneath the privilege and honor created especially for them. An authentic leader understands no one is better at being him than him, and he can never truly be himself if he has as a goal to be someone else. At the same time, authentic leaders understand the difference between modeling the good in others and striving to be someone else. Authentic leaders appreciate true authenticity is connected to a healthy self-worth and allows for a level of depth and connection with others not otherwise possible. Possessing self-worth, however, does not give you permission to look down upon others or to think more highly of yourself than you ought. Knowing the value of a healthy self-worth actually opens the door to discovering the value in others, but it first emanates from a place of honesty with oneself.

I contend much of the reason for an inability to embrace authenticity stems from a lack of honesty. Dishonesty promotes masking your true person, and a masked person cannot walk in complete authenticity. It is important to understand we are encouraged never to leave home without a mask. We rise each day and put on masks as part of our daily attire. We mask insecurities, pain, hurt, disappointment, failures, inabilities, shortcomings, prejudices, racism, sexism, jealousy, envy, and even strife. We often mask by living outside of our financial, emotional, and social means. The truth is we often mask our brokenness to the detriment of others. The outcome for leaders is an inability to connect with others at an authentic level, which often leads to damage and hurt not just to you as a leader but others as well.

The fact is we have worn masks for so long around so many issues of life that we are unaware we wear a mask. We have been lulled into believing the mask is our true person. But authenticity offers us an opportunity to get real with ourselves and begin to remove the blinders from our eyes and confront the masks we wear for the purpose of tearing them down and tearing them off. Authenticity carries a level of freedom unavailable otherwise, and the more masks we remove the more authenticity and transparency become accessible. As a result, we are more apt to effect true change within ourselves thereby inspiring change in others.

Authenticity is also the place where true leaders begin to build trust with others. In fact, they appreciate trust and its protection; these are critical elements to a leader's success. Leaders build trust with others, and trust paves the way for loyalty. Leaders who garner the trust and loyalty of others accomplish far beyond their expectations and own personal ability, as trust also carries power. In short, trust affects beliefs and behaviors. One who is authentic is considered by others as reliable and trustworthy. As such, others are much more apt to follow where such a leader goes. Moreover, leaders who are trusted have the support of those who will go the extra mile for the leader's success. Truthfully, in the relay of life, authenticity is the forerunner and first critical step to transparency.

In my own life as a leader, I have learned the value in authenticity by studying more about who I am at the core and by sharing more truths about the person I am with others. In addition, I have endeavored to be more honest with self and others in an effort to share more accurately the person I am from the inside out. In doing so, I have made every effort to remove the masks I was trained and groomed to believe I needed to wear. As such, I have learned an extra measure of integrity becomes accessible where a new level of vulnerability is present with others. Moreover, vulnerability with others paves the way for others to share more genuinely of themselves. In short, when others are able to observe their leader as one who is open to truth and vulnerability, they too are apt to follow suit. More importantly, I advocate allowing yourself to grow authentically allows you to become more appealing to others as a leader.

Transparency

> *Truth gives power to transparency.*

Random House Webster's College Dictionary defines transparent as "having the property of transmitting rays of light through its substance so that bodies situated beyond or behind can be distinctly seen." Transparent leaders operate from a place that allows the light of their innermost selves to be seen by others, as they are marked by the uncanny ability to be candid and open. Their light is powered by a value system that causes them to lead with straight, honest talk and fair dealing. More importantly, they understand there can be no transparency without authenticity and an unwavering decision to walk and operate in authentic ways. Transparency fueled by authenticity gives way to greater access to the inner person. Greater access to the inner woman or inner man inspires greater self-awareness and greater self-understanding. Armed with an inner knowledge, the leader is prepared to exercise a new level of self-discipline, self-development, and self-disclosure. She is ready for the transforming work that can only occur from the inside out, and she is fully aware true transparency is transformative.

Authentic leaders understand the ability to walk in transparency is fueled by a commitment to truth. One who walks outside of truth diminishes his capacity to live transparently. In fact, one who walks outside of truth often lives in fear of being uncovered and, in turn, loses the ability to be vulnerable with others. Truly transparent leaders seek after truth with a goal to dwell in truth and its liberating power while allowing truth to dwell within them. Truth and transparency carry a certain freedom empowering a leader to operate at an entirely new level of leadership effectiveness and impact.

Even more compelling, transparency and the work that makes it real have the power to influence and impact those who come after the leader and who choose to embrace authentic relationships with authentic leaders. In that space, they can see transformative work in others and also be inspired toward their own journey to inside out transforming work. Living a life of transparency allows the leader to be who he says he is. It is, in essence, the next level of authenticity. There is very little more critical to followers than a genuine leader whom they can trust and who is who he says he is and who does what he says he will do.

In your own leadership journey, consider the following challenge: Think about three leaders from your past. Can you say unequivocally that at least one of them was transparent in his leadership? Was that person committed to truth, honesty, self-awareness, and self-understanding? Did he or she live by a value system that promoted straight talk and fair dealing with others? Did this leader strive to live a life that was unmasked by inauthenticity? Now think about your own life in leadership. How would you describe your ability to live transparently? What lessons have you learned about the importance of transparency, and how will you apply those lessons to your leadership walk going forward?

Influence

> *The greatest leaders exercise leadership in an ethical manner and uplift others.*

Whether realized or not, influence carries with it a great deal of power—that is, power to produce results. Moreover, influential leaders recognize influence is not haphazard and, therefore, have a strategy around exercising their influence. First, however, the most influential leaders recognize they, too, are influenced by others. As such, the best leaders are careful in selecting relationships and fully comprehend every leader requires a leader, or a confidant—someone who will hold him accountable and speak loving truth into his life (albeit it may hurt at times). In other words, they understand influence is outcome determinative for the greatest leaders.

Properly exercised influence will greatly affect a leader's followers as well as others who are part of his sphere of influence. Every leader possesses a sphere of influence even if she has not taken the time to understand who is a part of her sphere. By definition, a leader's sphere of influence consists of those with which the leader carries a great deal of persuasive power. What the leader says and does plays a significant role in the decisions made by those within her sphere. Truly influential leaders strive to know and/or understand those within their sphere of influence.[7] Such understanding gives them a better opportunity to build greater relationships, greater leadership skills, and thus greater outcomes. In addition, a leader's sphere of influence is not stagnant but carries the ability to be fluid. Much of its fluidity, however, will depend on how the leader approaches influence. Great leaders seek to increase their sphere of influence in order to have a greater positive impact on a greater audience.

More important, and understanding the significance of their influence, genuine leaders take to heart their responsibility and accountability around their value system. They purposely live into their values and maintain core values that guide their lives and their leadership, and they understand integrity helps the leader live into his value system.

---

[7] A leader may not always have the luxury of personally knowing those who are a part of her sphere of influence. However, where possible, to glean at least some demographic information would be helpful, as it will allow the leader to operate from a place of knowledge and, for the greatest leaders, wisdom.

Influential leaders are also willing to commit to creative ways of holding themselves accountable to the value system by which they purport to live. By doing so, they will more rapidly internalize their values. Internalized values are the values by which we live. Values that are not internalized will not surface when our backs are up against a wall. As an example, one of my closest friends and I recently committed our individual value systems to a written work. We shared our written values with one another and agreed we would stand as accountability partners one with the other around our commitment to live and lead from a place of integrity as related to our values. We both understand values that have been internalized come forth from the inside out. A value system is not like a cloak one takes off and puts on as is convenient for the current situation. Rather, values are lived out on a daily basis because true values embody the leader causing the leader to be embodied by values that originate from his core.

Influential leaders like the greatest athletes understand the critical nature of a strong core. When one's core is strengthened, one naturally has greater overall strength. I learned this lesson from my recent personal training activities. In short, two years ago I committed to working on the body aspect of my holistic self (mind, body, and spirit). So I got serious about going to the gym and working out regularly (five times per week). I thought I was doing well, but when I decided to get a personal trainer she helped me strengthen my core in ways I had not previously experienced. As a result, I have now found firsthand how strengthening my physical core has helped to strengthen my body overall. In addition, strengthening my core physical body has helped me to have greater focus of mind and spirit development. It has made a tremendous difference not just in my physical appearance but also in my presence when I am with others. Try it. You might achieve some of the same types of amazing results I have experienced.

Finally, truly influential leaders, also like great athletes, know in order to "win the game" they must operate from a position of strength. The greatest leaders know, understand, and strive toward this end. As an example of core values chosen by my friend and I, one of us selected goodness while the other selected humility. Importantly, we have given each other permission to call to one another's attention conduct or behaviors that fall outside of the values to which we each committed, thus providing even greater incentive for us to be true to our stated values. As a reminder, remember that ethical influence is closely tied to morality and living justly in relation to your commitment as a leader in service to others. Before exercising your influence as a leader, consider its true implications against a bona fide integrity-based value system.

Impact

> The best leaders have impact as an ultimate goal for their lives as leaders.

Many people go through life not fully appreciating the impact (negative or positive) they have had on the lives of others. Truly impactful leaders, however, lead from a place of intentionality, authenticity, and transparency, understanding the strength of their influence and the ultimate value of their impact. Impactful leaders do not simply drive change and, in fact, understand the ineffectiveness of change for the sake of change. Rather, genuinely impactful leaders drive to make a difference—the kind of difference that has the power to positively impact the lives of others. Therefore, I contend, their goal is positive, life transforming impact.

While influence and impact have a great deal in common, impact carries influence to yet another level. These leaders commit themselves to great integrity and aim high toward creating a lasting legacy that will outlive their earthly lives (an inheritance for those who come after). Further, they understand impact equals legacy, and if legacy is an inheritance then they are driven by the very possibility of leaving behind for future leaders valuable lessons that will cause them to become impactful leaders as well. An unknown author once said, "Give a man a fish and you have fed him for today. Teach a man to fish and you have fed him for a lifetime." Impactful leaders are compelled by this truth. Moreover, wasn't this method utilized by Jesus when He sent the disciples (His original followers) out to become "fishers of men"? He taught them; in turn, they taught others causing His legacy to live on and on and on...

By way of further illustration, once a person passes away, many people ask this question: What did he or she do with his or her dash? As explained in Chapter 1, the dash is the punctuation used between a person's birth year and year of death to signify the time during which that person lived. In essence, it is the time one has been given to journey through life: the time one is given to make a positive contribution to a world from which we each take so much. The impact of a dash can outlive a person or pass with insignificance upon one's death. Not every leader can claim positive impact, yet every leader should claim the desire and commitment to work to achieve impact. By way of example, Martin Luther King Jr. was a leader of great impact. Rosa Parks was a leader of great impact. Mahatma Gandhi was a leader of great impact. John F. Kennedy was a leader of great impact. Nelson Mandela is a leader of great impact. Each of these leaders accomplished a legacy that has outlived or will outlive them, as the lives of untold numbers of people have been positively impacted by the work and leadership of these leaders. Achieving impact, however, is not defined solely by numbers. Rather, impact is defined by the depth of influence a leader has on those who follow. The key is that the positive impact is life altering (transforming) for those who follow.

Take some time in your own journey to consider leaders you believe have had a great impact. Reflect upon what made them impactful as a leader. Ask yourself this question: What impact do I desire to create in my life as a leader? If your aim as leader is not toward legacy, you are cordially invited to raise your bar, as legacy is the level of impact to which the best leaders aspire.

IMPORTANT MILE MARKERS IN INTEGRITY-BASED LEADERSHIP

— When intention meets purpose, it sets the stage for transformation.

— Authentic leaders choose depth over facade and truth over deceit.

— Transparency fueled by authenticity allows greater access to the inner person.

— Influential leaders strive to know those within their sphere of influence.

— Impactful leaders strive to make a positive difference.

Chapter 6

THE ART OF SETTING AND ACHIEVING GOALS

The essence of leadership, as you learned at the outset, is relational, connectional, and sacrificial. Parenthetically, the best leadership is also intergenerational. As I come to the close of the substantive portions of this work, however, and before turning to the more practical, I am compelled to revisit my original definition of the term *leadership*. As you know, as early as Chapter 1, I said that leadership is the art of ethically influencing others to move toward a particular goal or specific achievement and is marked by intentionality and an attitude of service. While this definition is clearly workable, it no longer completely satisfies the leader into which I have been transformed as a result of this project and my current work. Leadership, as I now more fully understand, is the gift of sacrifice for the enrichment of "another." Now that leadership has been more clearly and succinctly defined, my hope is that you as a leader will strongly consider what sacrifice you are willing to make on behalf of others. For this is the true mark of a leader who is destined to not only reach the finish line but also break through the finish line leaving a legacy for those who follow.

More importantly, since you have now come to understand the true meaning of leadership, the importance in personal or experiential formation, the power of legacy mapping, and the significance of adopting the Integrity-Based Leadership Model (IBLM), you might logically ask yourself, what's next? What am I being summoned to undertake on the road to living into authentic leadership and finding my greatest leadership contribution? Your next leg of the journey requires a decision in the form of commitment followed by action. There can be no real advancement or improvement on your journey unless first you make a personal, committed decision and then take some specific action toward the goal of becoming a leader of legacy accomplished through sacrifice. By take action I mean address with specificity areas in your leadership walk that you desire or, better, understand need to be moved to the next level. As with any area where a growth opportunity exists, you must be willing to take the necessary actions to move from where you are to higher ground.

Leaders who make a difference give their best to their leadership call. To do so not only requires sacrifice but also focus coupled with a plan. I suggest following the SAAG principle: setting and achieving goals. If a leader does not know where he is headed, any road will take him there.

However, a focused plan around your call promises to result in much greater contributions to the lives of others. Even if you are a leader who has established a plan for your leadership, I suggest this is a great time to revisit your plan, especially in light of all you have learned about answering your life's call. In fact, I advocate that this is a great time to revisit your life as leader in conjunction with the leadership path set out in this work. Once your path is clearly defined, then your next step is to set forth your goals in written form together with a specific plan on how those goals will be attained. Think about securing the services of a facilitator whose responsibility will be to challenge you to set realistic, achievable, and measureable goals. Earlier this year, I did just that. I spent two days with a brilliant facilitator who helped me redefine who I am as a leader and commit to writing what I intended to complete during the next two years. The book you are holding in your hand right now is one of the accomplishments of this year. Consequently, I am certain this process works.

Finally, the walk of leadership promises to hold its challenges. In fact, it would not be true leadership if it did not. Further, and as you have probably already experienced, there will be times when your greatest desire is to throw up your hands and walk away. If you are truly called to leadership, however, giving up is not an option. Rather, as you are faced with mounting challenges, consider a spiritually grounded course of action, including the following: identify, attack, overcome, victory.

Identify

To identify/name or call out an area of struggle, opportunity, or place for personal improvement in your life as leader creates the pathway toward greater self-awareness, self-development, and self-improvement. An identification serves as an acknowledgment and opens the door for honesty with yourself, understanding there can be no honesty with others until you walk honestly with yourself. Consider this: *Anything* that prevents you from becoming an intentional leader who walks in authenticity and transparency or otherwise inhibits your journey to greatness can be classified as an adversary. An adversary has the responsibility of serving as an opponent whose main task is to preclude you from attaining your leadership goals. The acknowledgment of the areas in which you need improvement or growth allows you to serve notice on the adversary of your commitment to do the required work to realize your greatest leadership contribution. To uncover your greatest leadership contribution, you must be intentional about self-reflection, self-discovery, and uncovering true purpose. Such goals are attained only through intentional conduct geared toward finding where your piece fits in the puzzle of life. Take the opportunity to look at this book as your invitation to identify where you would like to grow and begin the process of moving from your current status to a new level of leadership. Move into a quiet space, shut out some of the noise of life, and listen. You will be surprised as to how much you learn. Moreover, be open to the idea of listening to others. Oftentimes others are capable of seeing things in us that we cannot see in ourselves.

Attack

Too often we spend our time attacking others rather than addressing our own human frailties. We spend too much time pointing out what is wrong with someone else while failing to examine ourselves. To attack, as referred to in this writing, contemplates once and for all coming face-to-face with your opportunity for growth—an aggressive move toward the adversary or attack with the intent to destroy the enemy. Often we think of an enemy or adversary as a person who desires to see us fail. While such a statement may carry some truth, consider yourself challenged to focus not on others but on your own internal enemy that has inhibited you from growing in leadership. To attack is to focus on dismantling from the inside out the personal effects that have inhibited you from intentionality in your leadership journey and walking in complete authenticity and transparency. Ask yourself what personal peculiarities, habits, or leadership traits you possess. Are they inhibitors or facilitators of your leadership success? Do they serve as oxygen to enhance the life of someone else? Have you led others from your own place of pain or discontent? Or have you taken the time to address the things that have caused you pain to avoid even the possibility of causing similar pain and hurt to someone else?

Getting real with self is the first step in facing your opportunities for growth and development. Once you get real with yourself, the easier it will be to begin the process of "attacking" the internal adversary that works to thwart your hard effort toward developing into a transforming leader. Along the way, there is one critical item for you to keep in mind. This process is not about attacking yourself (or anyone else for that matter); rather, it is about attacking the issue or opportunity that limits or has limited your ability to grow and develop as a leader.

Overcome

To overcome means to prevail over, conquer, beat, or overpower. It is the step prior to victory, as victory is not possible until first we conquer or beat an opponent. When you have worked to overcome the adversary that prevents or has prevented you from growing in leadership grace, you begin the process of living a different leadership life. As an overcomer, you now regularly assess your commitment to intentionality. You understand from the inside out the necessity to be intentional about leadership; intentional about living a life of service to others; intentional about moral and ethical conduct; intentional about self-examination, self-understanding, and self-improvement; intentional about adopting new thinking and behaviors; intentional about finding the appropriate resources to assist you in your areas of opportunity; intentional about how you ethically persuade or stimulate those within your sphere of influence; and intentional about an attitude, demeanor, and behavior that will positively impact the lives of others.

Another important aspect of overcoming has to do with what we confess, profess, declare, and believe. In fact, I believe boldly telling our own story will help us overcome. We must begin by speaking in the positive and speaking our leadership desires. We must begin to speak and believe that we have overcome the things that have previously kept us bound and unable to reach the level of transforming leadership. Not only must we speak positively, but we also must believe in the power of overcoming. We must speak positively and tell our stories even when we have not seen the entire fruit of that on which we are working; we must continue to believe and speak life into it until it comes to pass. We must continue to walk in it believing. Then after it is done, after it is over, after we have overcome, after we have conquered, then we must tell others continually. We must continually tell others and show others how they too can overcome and walk in victory. We must help them see they can become transformed leaders by overcoming that which has previously stood in their pathway blocking their ability to become. So whatever it is, what you think and how you act or react make a difference. Learn to walk in the way of overcoming.

Victory

By the time you reach victory, you have attained sustainable leadership growth. While overcoming is great, you must keep your eyes fixed on the ultimate outcome: walking in victory. To walk in victory means you are no longer bound by the limits you previously placed on yourself and your leadership contributions. Victory means you are now on the path to creating a legacy for those who come behind. Victory means you now have the faith to believe all things are possible to the one who believes. Victory means you now have the capacity to really impact the lives of others.

III

BREAKING THROUGH
THE FINISH LINE

Chapter 7

CENTERING FOR THE JOURNEY

This chapter is entitled "Centering for the Journey" because that is exactly what it takes. If your desire is toward achieving a greater level of impact through leadership, you must remain centered, focused, and intentional about the person you are from the inside out. To help you in this regard, this chapter contains twelve meditations geared to help with your leadership walk. The meditations each correspond to a word or phrase that typifies the lesson to be learned or gained from the meditation. Try putting them to work on your own leadership dash.

Before taking up the twelve leadership meditations, however, consider the following questions: (1) Why are you on this journey? (2) What fruit have you produced in your life as a leader? (3) What have you done to embrace integrity as a value for your leadership? (4) What outcomes are you committed to accomplishing both now and going forward? During or after completing the meditations, what specific plan will you put in place to reach your identified outcomes? That is, what will you put in place to help you achieve your Integrity-Based Leadership Model (IBLM) outcomes.

The twelve meditations each correspond to a particular lesson as identified by the following list:

1. Faith
2. Facing Challenge
3. Living Just
4. Humility
5. Courage
6. Purpose

7. Ethical Mind-Set
8. Power of the Tongue
9. Forgiveness
10. Encouragement
11. Wisdom
12. Endurance

Meditation 1   ***FAITH***

Faith Is Your Sustenance!

If you can believe, all things are possible
to him who believes.
(MARK 9:23, NKJV)

Take the first step in faith. You don't have to see the
whole staircase, just take the first step.
—DR. MARTIN LUTHER KING JR.

A mind troubled by doubt cannot focus
on the course to victory.
—ARTHUR GOLDEN

Scripture records performance of many miracles during Jesus' life on earth. Each of those miracles required a measure of faith for their fulfillment. The same can be said for your life today and what is required of you to become the leader you were intended to be. One of the hardest things to do in life is to be effective as a leader. There are many people in the world who enjoy the title leader, yet not all of them have enjoyed leadership success. In fact, there are many people who *unknowingly* serve as leaders (diminishing their capacity to be intentional about leadership). This is true because a leader, in general terms, is anyone who is privileged to have followers. The sign of

121

a true leader, however, is not found simply in the fact that others will follow. True leadership goes far beyond a casual encounter with admirers who might be tempted to mimic what you do. Leadership is a gift not to be taken for granted. It is not a mantle or badge to be worn. It is not a cloak that is put on and taken off when convenient. Leadership is serious business, and it is found in the positive impact the leader produces in the lives of others. For these reasons, this meditation seeks to reach "intentional leaders"—the ones who know without a doubt that leadership is the office to which they have been summoned and the clarion call to which they have responded: "Here am I. Send me."

True leadership is not achieved in a vacuum, and the journey to bona fide leadership will require an extra measure of faith. You must believe even when others have resorted to fear and doubt. You must believe the impossible in order to achieve the extraordinary. You must believe in yourself and others even when having faith defies logic. You must teach others the art of believing and the discipline of faith. You must know the disappointment of dreams deferred as well as the hope of ideals realized. As a great leader, you must understand faith is your sustenance; it is the fuel that keeps you pressing toward the mark and destiny to which you have been called. It is your connection between what is and what will be. You must exhibit faith in your God, faith in yourself, and faith in the ability of the community to stay the course. Above all, you must understand faith is your belief in the possibility of what has not yet been seen. If you can see it

or completely conceive it, you have not yet fully compre-
hended the true meaning of faith. Faith is not simply your
sustenance, faith is your sustainer, and faith points you to
your source. In fact, great leaders understand the difference
between "the source" and a resource. The source is God who
has "not given us the spirit of fear, but of power, love and
sound mind" (2 Timothy 1:7, KJV). A resource possesses
only limited ability, while God, your source, has power to
do the impossible and help you achieve the unfathomable.

One of the greatest examples of true leadership was
found in Dr. Martin Luther King Jr. Dr. King had the audac-
ity to have faith that true equality would and could become
a part of the fabric of America. King knew the America of
old would be transformed even if it was destined to occur
outside of his lifetime. In fact, he was a true visionary leader
who spent much of his time articulating a worldview that was
quite contrary to the times in which he lived. This unique
mark has set him apart from so many leaders before, during,
and subsequent to his time. True to his faith and message,
King did not waste time stuck on things that were not. No, he
focused his sight and his faith on the possibilities for which
he dreamed and spoke of in the form of amazing vision. King
also developed a unique and personal brand and a legacy that
lives even today. Like King, you must believe so much so that
you can look your enemy in the face and declare victory over
the things to which you put your mind and your hands. You
must also be prepared to walk outside your comfort zone.
Know this: Leaders speak life and declare victory in the lives

of others. Great leaders make a difference, and it is the kind of difference that positively impacts the lives of others.

MEDITATION CHALLENGE: In your own life, identify a leader who has shown his or her ability to set a vision and keep the faith on the road to achieving a dream. To set vision, a leader must first see it, feel it, believe it, breathe life into it, and participate in the pursuits that will bring the vision into reality, all the while maintaining a strong faith—an absolute on any journey to creating legacy out of your dash.

The questions for you to contemplate in this first meditation of your journey are as follows: Where is your faith, and in whom do you believe? Do you believe the Word of God or not? Whatever situation you face, God is able to carry you through to the victory that is already yours by virtue of your inheritance. Whatever leadership challenge you face, you must believe the battle has already been won and that victory is at hand.

— — — —

As you are tempted to walk in unbelief, remind yourself of God's promise that "all things are possible to him who believes."

Meditation 2 **FACING CHALLENGE**

Be Prepared for the Attacks!

No weapon that is formed against you
shall prosper, and every tongue which rises
against you in judgment you shall condemn.
This is the heritage of the servants of the Lord and
their righteousness is from me, says the Lord.
(ISAIAH 54:17, NKJV)

In times of storm, the shallowness of the
root structure is revealed.
—AUTHOR UNKNOWN

Leadership is challenging! So many people focus on the glam and glory of leadership, yet they fail to understand the sacrifices and challenges that accompany those who occupy positions of leadership. When you first embarked upon your role as leader, you probably had no idea about the attacks, the criticism, the responsibility, and the enormous accountability. You, like many in all probability, were focused on your success and the authority part of leadership, ignoring that with the success and authority came a whole family of extras. You are probably saying to yourself right now: Why in the world did I agree to take this position? I didn't sign up for this. Well, I have news for you. If you signed up to be a leader, you signed up for all of the above and more. Leadership is not designed to be easy. Leadership is not designed to be a walk in the park. Leadership is not designed to be a place where you collect a healthy paycheck, become self-absorbed, and simply take in all of your accolades. Leadership is also not the place where you should be overcome with self-pride. Leadership is the place of humility and service, and the greatest of leaders have learned and come to embody this truth. Leadership is designed to challenge you at the core of your very being. Leadership is designed to force you to ask tough questions, to face tough people and tough situations, and to confront the recurring challenges not only in your profession but also in your personal life and yes in the lives of others.

Leadership can make you or break you. It really is up to you. Much of it depends on how you face the challenges that are intimately connected to your position. Think about it in this way: When you are assigned to a position of leadership, you will have others assigned to follow you. You will, in essence, become responsible for their direction, their work, their development, and their outcomes (at least as it relates to the area of their lives wherein you are their leader). Don't you think with this kind of responsibility for others executing with excellence will be difficult? Don't you think you should be challenged to give and do your best? Don't you think others will be critical of you? Don't you think it really is about them and not about you? Leadership really is your challenge to see how high you can raise the banner for someone other than yourself—even in the face of hardship or all out battle. To be an effective leader, you must know what to take to heart and what to simply let go. You must be prepared to face conflict and resolve differences. You must refuse to operate on assumptions or to be immobilized, or walk in trepidation, or anger, or frustration, or bitterness.

You must understand, exercise wisdom and restraint, and recognize as a child of God that, yes, weapons will be formed against you, but God has things under control. Those weapons just won't prosper. Recall that weapons were formed against Jesus and every other man or woman who chose the path of great leadership. In fact, those weapons will make you stronger and more effective if only you learn to use them as tools and not see them as weapons. Stop focusing on the weapons that have been formed against you, and in the name of the almighty Creator call down those tongues that speak against you in judgment. Take a long look at yourself, and see where you could use further development and ask God to help you grow. Once you have asked God to help you grow, begin to look for resources that will lift you and your leadership to the next level of challenges. Use the resources to stimulate your growth and development.

The question for you in this second meditation of the journey is as follows: Can you take an honest, personal inventory of how you have responded to those who have raised weapons (roadblocks and attacks) against you?

MEDITATION CHALLENGE: Think of someone who has formed a weapon against you; condemn that weapon and the words of the tongue that have risen against you. Forgive the person who formed the weapon or spoke those words, pray for them, and let it go. There is much work ahead on your leadership journey, and there is no time to be stalled, thwarted, stuck, or set back by holding a grudge. The freedom comes from forgiving and letting go.

— — — —

When you face challenges in your leadership, instead of drinking from the cup of bitterness, use those challenges as opportunities to take spiritual authority over the enemy that seeks to destroy you. And remember, it is written, "no weapon that is formed against you shall prosper."

Meditation 3   ***LIVING JUST***

Roll Up Your Sleeves

For everyone to whom much is given, from him much will be required; and to whom much has been committed, of him they will ask the more.
(LUKE 12:48B, NKJV)

Unless a man undertakes more than he possibly can do, he will never do all that he can.
—HENRY DRUMMOND

Congratulations! You have reached your goal of becoming a leader. Now roll up your sleeves because the hard work is about to begin. Leadership is serious business. Are you ready to leave your ego behind and walk in humility? Are you ready to work alongside others? Are you ready to serve others? Are you ready to help others find and reach their greatest potential? Are you ready to set an example for others? Are you ready to bring others along? Are you ready to walk in integrity and with purpose? Are you ready to sacrifice for the benefit of others? Are you ready to make a contribution that will make a difference in the world? Are you ready to think outside the norm and with far greater depth in order to foster an uncommon, life-changing walk among others? Are you truly ready?

Scripture tells us to whom much is given much will be required. Yes, that means you. If you have been elevated to a position of leadership, whether or not you have amassed great personal wealth, much has been given to you. What you do with it is yours to decide. My advice is to cherish it; roll up your sleeves and get to work. Get to work making a difference in someone else's life. It will make all of the difference in yours. Get to work loving someone who you really do not think is lovable. It will cause others to share love with you and open the pathway for unmerited favor. Get to work educating someone who our system has failed remembering words of Scripture, "as you did it to one of the least of these my brothers, you did it to me" (Matthew 25:40, ESV). Get to work raising someone else's social conscience so they can get to work giving back to this great world from which we each take so much. Get to work remembering your own responsibility in this regard:

> The Spirit of the Lord is upon me, because he has anointed me to proclaim good news to the poor. He has sent me to proclaim liberty to the captives and recovering of sight to the blind, to set at liberty those who are oppressed, to proclaim the year of the Lord's favor (Luke 4:18–19, ESV).

Get to work raising your standard for excellence; it will inspire others on their own journey to legacy. You must be self-motivated and exercise decided and extraordinary self-discipline and understand mediocrity is no longer an option. You must give the best of you and know what you know. But more importantly know what you don't. Understand your limitations. Don't be ashamed or afraid to seek out the help you both need and desire. Be and become the best you can be. When you have reached what you perceive as your limit, dig deeper. It will expand your capacity, and you will learn to lean not on your own limited understanding but on the power that is within, given as a gift from the giver of life. It is God who takes the ordinary and achieves the impossible so that others might experience the extraordinary.

Make a decision today about your leadership contribution and then roll up your sleeves and begin the work. Stretch yourself beyond your usual limits. Remember that God begins the real work at the outer limits of your comfort zone. When you get outside of your comfort zone, you are moving to your place of weakness, and you are assured in 2 Corinthians 12:9 that God's strength is made perfect in your weakness. Set your sights on a leadership goal that reaches far beyond your comfort zone. Imagine your greatest contribution making and having an astonishing impact on the lives and well-being of others. Then march right up to the edge of your place of comfort and let go... in faith. After all, you are a leader—are you not?

What will you release today? What will you do to add value to someone else's life with the expectation of getting nothing in return but the satisfaction of knowing your presence and power helped and influenced someone today?

MEDITATION CHALLENGE: Challenge yourself to develop a specific thought, idea, or plan on how you will consistently show leadership by regularly making a conscious and deliberate contribution of time and talent to the life or lives of others. By the way, great leaders understand the concept of great stewardship.

— — — —

Remember that God has given you much, but what you have received is not simply for you to indulge and enjoy. Now our global community has need of thee and of you much is required.

Meditation 4   *HUMILITY*

Be Careful!

For I say, through the grace given to me,
to everyone who is among you, not to
think of himself more highly than he ought
to think, but to think soberly, as God has
dealt to each one a measure of faith.
(ROMANS 12:3, NKJV)

We come nearest to the great when
we are great in humility.
—RABINDRANATH TAGORE

Have you checked your humility meter lately? All too often those in positions of leadership think of themselves as above those they lead and everyone else for that matter. I am sure you are saying to yourself, Not me. I am not like other leaders. But before you speak so fast, answer the following questions about your leadership style so that you will have a glimpse into your "humility meter." Do you introduce or define yourself by your title or what you do for a living? Does your job description include quietly serving the needs of others? In your position as leader, do you consider the needs of others even when they differ from your own? Do you speak regularly on behalf of those who cannot or do not have the luxury of speaking on behalf of themselves? When is the last time you did a pro bono project or gave service to a community organization? When is the last time you went the extra mile to make a difference in the lives of others? Do you manage others or create an environment wherein others are empowered to reach their own leadership potential? As leaders, we must begin to dispel any notion suggesting we are more than, better than, or other than those we have been called upon to lead. The office of leader is an office of service. Looking again at the life and story of Jesus, He was the perfect example of service in leadership. His humility was carried out in His willingness to endure the shame of the cross not for Himself but for humankind. When is the last time you bore a cross on someone else's behalf?

As leaders, it is critical for us to understand the value in others. It is also important to refrain from self-absorption, selfish behaviors, and self-serving conduct. We need not brag or boast. Rather, we are called upon to walk in humility. A humble heart paves the way for an extraordinary life and model of leadership. A leader's ability to create legacy will be severely limited where the leader's focus is set on him and him alone. Self-absorption is a blinder that prevents a leader from seeing others as well as the roadblocks of life that thwart clear and life-transforming vision.

The question to ponder is this: How do you know when one has led well? First, leadership is ex post facto—that is, whether or not one has led well will only be fully known after the act of leadership has been fulfilled. For certain, the one who has led well has led from a place of sacrifice and humility. He is the one who has pursued that which is good, ethical, just, and moral. And a humble leader will have avoided shallow water thinking. The humble leader has also divorced himself from ego and understands the connection between humility and an authentic and transparent life of leadership.

Our meditation Scripture points out the importance of remaining sober minded in relation to one's accomplishments. When we become enthralled with who we are and what we have done, it clouds our view of who God is and what He has called us to be. It limits our thinking and our ability to think outside the ego-driven box in which we exist. It limits God's ability to take our little and make it into much on behalf of many. Examine history and the experiences in your own life. Have not the greatest of these been those who have walked in a spirit of humility, who were kindhearted, and who were determined to make a difference in the lives of others? The greatest accomplishment is not what we do for ourselves and make known to others. Rather, the greatest accomplishment is found in the quiet deposits we make in the lives of others. Matthew 6:3–4 (NKJV) reminds us, "But when you do a charitable deed, do not let your left hand know what your right hand is doing, that your charitable deed may be in secret; and your Father who sees in secret will Himself reward you openly."

MEDITATION CHALLENGE: Ask yourself the tough question about where you measure on the humility meter.

After careful deliberation, consider asking someone you know who will speak in honesty their impression of how you measure on the humility meter. Thereafter, challenge yourself to show up wherever you are required to be not in the "largeness" of who you are but in the humility to which you are being called. Record the experience of how you are received by others and what you are now in a position to accomplish.

— — — —

The very next time you are tempted to boast, brag, or think more highly of yourself than you ought to, remember the glory belongs to God, and a humble heart is a heart after God's.

Meditation 5   ***COURAGE***

Who Promised You Comfort?

*In the world you will have tribulation; but be
of good cheer, I have overcome the world.*
(JOHN 16:33B, NKJV)

*For the days will come upon you when your
enemies will build an embankment around you,
surround you and close you in on every side.*
(LUKE 19:43, NKJV)

*Courage is being scared to death—
but saddling up anyway.*
—JOHN WAYNE

So many leaders have made the mistake of thinking once they reach a position of leadership they can kick back, put up their heels, and take a rest. But I have news for you: Taking on a position of leadership means all the more you must roll up your sleeves and get in the game. So you ask, what does it mean to get in the game? Being in a position of leadership means you understand behind every corner there lurks an enemy awaiting the opportunity to take you out. In fact, the enemy's job is to set you up to believe the hard work is behind you on that long road you traveled to reach your place of leadership. As usual, the enemy is a liar. The hard work is ahead. The sacrifice is ahead, and the reward is in serving others so they may reach their own place of destiny. Moreover, when you decide to move from the place of comfort to a place of serving others, it clears the pathway for you to walk among the greatest of leaders and opens the doors for you to receive. Does not the Scripture teach the law of sowing and reaping? "Do not be deceived: God is not mocked, for whatever one sows, that will he also reap" (Galatians 6:7, ESV).

Sowing seeds of great leadership does not transpire at the place of comfort. History reveals countless numbers of leaders who understood great leadership begins beyond one's place of comfort. In fact, I am afraid if you are right now sitting in comfort you have not fully challenged yourself as a leader. If you have no enemies or attackers, then you are operating from a place of comfort.

Every great leader has both attackers and enemies. But the greatest of leaders understand the responsibility of responding to them from a place of love, even though to do so might be uncomfortable. After all, who promised you comfort? In fact, I am afraid if you are operating out of comfort that you have not begun to live the extraordinary life of leadership that is available to you. What's more is if you step outside your place of comfort, you will open up the door for God to step in and lead you far beyond your leadership expectations. Look at the lives of people like Sojourner Truth, Nelson Mandela, John F. Kennedy, Mahatma Gandhi, Fannie Lou Hamer, and even Oprah Winfrey. Each of these leaders has made tremendous contributions to the lives of others while simultaneously making the choice to move beyond their own comfort in order to make a difference. In fact, they each lived or live in a manner that exemplified/ exemplifies getting outside of comfort is both risky and uncertain. It is, however, an absolute necessity.

How are you being challenged out of comfort into a place of sacrifice and service? It is time to make up in your mind that you are going to take your focus off of comfort and redirect your leadership desires toward the building up of others. The world awaits you. The world both needs and desires leaders who are sold out for peace, justice, and the true liberation of all humankind. There is enough work to go around, and we need not be stagnated by envy, jealousy, and strife. Rather, we each are called to get in the game and make the contribution we were uniquely designed to make. Now make no mistake; the closer you come to finding your true place of leadership and the contribution you are called to make, the more severe the attack of the enemy will be. The enemy desires to keep you under attack so you lose courage to fulfill your leadership destiny. But like the leaders identified earlier, you must be prepared to face the attacks that come. Those attacks may be physical, mental, emotional, or even psychological, but you are more than an overcomer. Don't be deterred from your leadership destiny, and remember the road to your destiny is paved by a journey. Your courage to travel the journey must be intimately connected to your faith in God's ability to deliver you safely to the place of leadership already prepared for you.

Develop your own plan for stepping outside your zone of comfort. Before you will be able to make such an accomplishment, however, you must know very clearly the boundaries you have created for yourself. Perhaps you perceive a little tribulation waits just beyond the place of your comfort. Just remember our first Scripture of this meditation and know the longer you prolong moving out of comfort the longer you delay God's ability to do the extraordinary.

MEDITATION CHALLENGE: Do one thing this week to move from your place of comfort to a place of making one sacrifice on behalf of someone else. Try it again next week and the week after and the week after. Try it until it becomes a way of life. See how your impact will begin to grow.

— — — —

The next time you are tempted by the thought of comfort, remember that it is only temporary. Life has its challenges for all, so you might as well develop courage to get in the game and stay in the game. Your greatest reward is in reaching for your full leadership potential, which lurks beyond the place of comfort. When you have reached it, you will have impacted the lives of so many others.

Meditation 6 **PURPOSE**

God Wants a Stake in Your Game!

For I know the thoughts that I think toward you
says the Lord, thoughts of peace and not of evil,
to give you a future and a hope.
(JEREMIAH 29:11, NKJV)

The measure of life, after all,
is not its duration but its donation.
—CORRIE TEN BOOM

The purpose of life is a life of purpose.
—ROBERT BYRNE

I f you are on a leadership journey, you should have already asked yourself this question: Am I fulfilling the purpose for which I was called and created? Don't make the mistake of thinking you are in this world by accident or that you were not uniquely designed to fulfill a particular purpose in life. There is a reason for your existence, and it is the privilege of each of us to find our own road to purpose. If you have determined yours is in some facet of leadership, then rejoice and read on. If you are not sure, still rejoice and read on. If you have begun the soul searching process to find your true life's purpose, rejoice and read on. Perhaps you have asked yourself the purpose question over and over again. Well maybe, just maybe, you are seeking your answer in the wrong place. If you really want to know your purpose for living, consider asking the one who created you. God really does want a stake in your game, and, in fact, He wants to lead you on your journey to fulfilling the purpose He has for you. If you are anything like me, as you face the challenges of leadership you continually revisit the question relating to whether or not you are in the right place and doing the right thing. Perhaps like many you are attempting to fly your own leadership plane. After all, this is your first plane, and you certainly don't want to spend your time in the copilot's seat. Well, I have news for you: There is no better place to be than sitting as God's copilot. Relax and follow His instruction. In fact, I did not learn how to be an effective leader of others until I learned how to be an effective copilot to God. The thing to remember about the copilot is that he assists or relieves the pilot, but he is not in command.

Perhaps your response is that you have already asked your creator and you have not heard a response. Consider whether or not you might be in purpose-chasing mode. Have you slowed down long enough to hear your life's call? Sometimes the key is in quietly shutting out the noise of life so that you might hear what life is saying. This is much easier said than done because of how we have come to live life, but take up the challenge of finding some quiet time and a quiet space and meditate while you are in that space. When you leave that space, continue to listen to your life. Look at the places you frequent, the things outside of you that bring you joy, the kind of people and things that draw you as well as the people and things to which you are drawn, volunteer your time giving back, get involved in a project about which you have great passion or concern. Listen, listen, listen, and listen even more. Get in the habit of listening for life at all times no matter where you find yourself. Listen to conversations you have with others, listen to the conversations you have with yourself, and listen to the conversations between others. Listen and be open to receive. Life's goal is not to hide purpose from you. Life's goal is to call you and then usher you into your purpose. Your responsibility is to get into a place where you can absolutely hear the call.

MEDITATION CHALLENGE: Make up in your mind that you are going to embrace the suggestions of this meditation. Ask, seek, knock, listen, and when life speaks, be prepared to take up the challenge life is placing before you. Become a more critical thinker, and give your best to each day life gives you. Expand your dialogue with others, and do not be afraid to ask others what gifts they see displayed in you. Do not be afraid to connect with self and others.

— — — —

The next time you are tempted to start again on the journey of chasing purpose, challenge yourself to stop, be still, and shut out some of the noise of life. Take note of things that give you life and bring joy. Instead of focusing on yourself, turn your attention toward the needs of others.

143

Do something that falls outside your zone of comfort. Think, think, and then listen. Listen, listen, and think. Open your mind and begin to listen for the summons of life. Be assured that life will call. The key is you must be in a position and place to hear the call of life.

Meditation 7   ***ETHICAL MIND-SET***

Don't Fight Your Way to the Head of the Pack

A gift opens the way for the giver and ushers him [or her] into the presence of the great.
(PROVERBS 18:16, NIV)

The Lord doesn't ask about your ability, only about your availability; and if you prove your dependability, the Lord will increase your capability.
—AUTHOR UNKNOWN

Don't judge each day by the harvest you reap but by the seeds you plant.
—ROBERT LOUIS STEVENSON

Have you ever met someone who is fighting or has fought his way to the top? Anything goes regardless to the number of people on which he steps or who might become casualties of his reckless pursuits. If you have met such a person, perhaps your response mirrors my response when I encounter such individuals. The characteristics they display are simply unattractive. Moreover, getting to the top by any means necessary is not the mark of a true leader. In fact, it is the antithesis of authenticity

145

and integrity—key character traits of top leaders. What is more is such conduct is lacking in positive values, behaviors, and boundaries—also necessary elements for genuine leaders.

Recall Scripture records your gift will make room for you and lead you before the great. That means the way to reach your goal as a leader awaits you as you proceed authentically in the gift(s) that are present in your life while simultaneously walking intentionally with integrity and in transparency. Stepping on an-other to get to where you are going will hurt you as much as it is hurtful to others, for in life we really do reap what we sow.

Plain and simple, succeeding in leadership is about knowing who you are (formation at its best), recognizing your call, becoming unquestionably committed to your purpose, charting your pathway, and following your ethically written plan. Further, abandoning selfish gain in exchange for service and sacrifice on behalf of others can make all the difference. In other words, you can reach success without leaving a trail of victims along the way. More importantly, if your goals require causing harm or injury to others, perhaps it is time to rethink your goals or the path you have designated to attain them.

Yes, there are those who live by the philosophy that we exist in a dog-eat-dog world. The truth is such thinking will not get you very far and certainly not for very long. Attitudes of this proportion are not positioned to make a positive contribution and difference in our global community.

As a leader who desires to live differently, however, you have a choice, and no one deprives you of that choice but you. You can either choose to walk down a different path or join those who will do just about anything for selfish gain. Your chance of attracting greater success into your life is far more likely when you give your best to formation and proceed discerning true leadership is relational, connectional, and sacrificial. Moreover, the most powerful and impactful leadership is intergenerational and emanates from a place of integrity. But integrity can be passed on to future generations only by those who themselves walk in integrity.

On the pathway to legacy, integrity must be met by a commitment to a code of ethics. A code of ethics is unwavering responsibility to a moral compass. It is not waiting for someone else to design your moral fortitude, but it's making a decision at the outset to live by a set of values that meet the highest standards of humanity.

MEDITATION CHALLENGE: Dedicate some quality time to think about your integrity meter and moral compass. Your integrity meter measures the values you have set in place for truth in your life, and your moral compass measures what ethical boundaries you have established for achieving your goals. Commit to writing what you will and will not do on your upward climb in leadership. If you clearly define your boundaries beforehand, chances are the moment you are tempted otherwise you will be prompted to choose integrity and ethics over any other path.

— — — —

Take some time to meditate about your integrity meter and moral compass. Take a stab at writing down your code of ethics. After you have committed your code to writing, begin to daily measure your conduct against your written word. If you measure up, great! If you do not, begin immediately to move your conduct in line with what you have said about the way you will live.

Meditation 8   ***POWER OF THE TONGUE***

What You Say Matters!

Death and life are in the power of the tongue:
and they that love it shall eat the fruit thereof.
(PROVERBS 18:21, KJV)

A still tongue makes a wise head.
—TRADITIONAL PROVERB

When you have spoken the word, it reigns over you.
When it is unspoken you reign over it.
—ARABIAN PROVERB

Often we live our lives as if the above passage and proverbs carry no truth and no power. However, the fact is the tongue is a powerful weapon, and as a leader you must be exceedingly careful how you use your tongue or allow it to use you. Think about the people with whom you most often enjoy spending time. Think also about the people who have added the most value to your life and your positive development. You probably gained the least from those who used their tongues for negative purposes like gossiping, putting others down, discouraging others, finding fault, and derailing good ideas. On the contrary, it is likely you gained the greatest value from those who have

149

spoken positive, life-affirming messages into your spirit and who have wisely used words to challenge your thinking and your direction.

Words are used together to create the language and understanding of a particular community. Words are powerful tools that can make a tremendous difference in the development of self and others. And words must be taken seriously, undertaken wisely, and used for the building up of others rather than breaking down. Great leaders choose their words with care and exercise wisdom *prior* to a shared word.

As a leader, it is incumbent upon you to speak life into others by carrying a positive message and finding the most productive and affirming ways to bring out the best in others. Leaders are often like coaches who stand on the sidelines encouraging their team to victory. You can gain far more with an encouraging word than with a harsh tongue. Unfortunately, leaders do not always take time to choose their words wisely. Often in haste to get things done, a leader may not exercise the wisest interpersonal competence. The leadership lesson exists in your ability to honestly consider the times in your leadership journey where you could have been more judicious in your use of words while working with others. This is the exact point where authenticity and transparency are met on the road to integrity. Allow it to be a moment of truth in your own journey. Honestly speaking, I can think of times in my own walk as a leader wherein I have not exercised the most prudent use of words. The leadership victory for me was understanding those times, seriously reflecting upon my interpersonal communication choices, talking to others to get it right and in the ability to live differently thereafter.

MEDITATION CHALLENGE: Someone once said we have two ears and one mouth because we should listen twice as much as we speak. As a leader, it is tremendously important that you develop impeccable listening skills. Often those whom you lead will tell you exactly what they need, but you must be in a position to hear. Their words may not always be verbal, yet they are speaking. A great leader learns the art of listening not just with her ears but with her internal compass that will guide her to the appropriate response. Try your hand at listening more attentively to those you lead and doing so in opposition to the urge to speak. Then try responding in a gentle and understanding fashion. Include those you lead in important decisions and even allow them room to exercise their own gifts of leadership. Assist them in finding the best in themselves and then give them a venue to practice what they have discovered. I think you will be amazed at the quality of what you receive in return.

— — — —

When you are tempted to speak, try overriding your temptation and opting to listen. When you have heard from deep inside, remember what you have learned about true leadership and then respond from that place.

Who Have You Forgiven Today?

And whenever you stand praying,
if you have anything against anyone,
forgive him, that your Father in heaven
may also forgive you your trespasses.
(MARK 11:25, NKJV)

Therefore, as the elect of God, holy and beloved,
put on tender mercies, kindness, humility,
meekness, longsuffering; Bearing with one another,
and forgiving one another, if anyone has a
complaint against another; even as Christ
forgave you, so you also must do.
(COLOSSIANS 3:12–13, NKJV)

There is no life apart from God's love.
Therefore, there is no life apart from forgiveness,
for forgiveness is the seal, the mark, and the
proof of love. If we say we have love and cannot
walk in forgiveness, we deceive ourselves,
and our "love" is only a parody of the real thing.
—MERCY AIKEN

There is no revenge so complete as forgiveness.
—JOSH BILLINGS

So many leaders miss out on the abundance of life's blessings because they walk in unforgiveness and often, in fact, have a *spirit* of unforgiveness. But having the courage to forgive an-other's trespasses is one of the foremost marks of a true leader. One common mistake leaders make is in thinking their trespasser will suffer if the leader refuses to extend forgiveness. The truth is that whether or not the other suffers, the leader who walks in unforgiveness will. Accordingly, the best leaders are peaceable and strive to walk in peace and forgiveness with all humankind. There is one widespread misunderstanding about forgiveness I would like to clarify once and for all. Forgiveness is more about the one who extends the hand of forgiveness (he who forgives the trespasses of others) than being about the recipient (he who may or may not seek your forgiveness). Moreover, if you desire that forgiveness be extended to you, it is critical that you become generous in forgiving others. Unforgiveness is detrimental to the mind, body, and spirit. It is a breeding ground for illness. Forgiveness, however, has a cleansing effect and is a stress reliever. Try forgiving someone and letting it go. You will feel the impact of that dead weight as it is lifted from you.

Importantly and often the issue of unforgiveness for many is tied to an inability to receive forgiveness. One reason you may have difficulty receiving forgiveness is related to the fact you have failed to extend forgiveness. Who have you forgiven lately, especially among those who perhaps you do not feel are worthy of forgiveness? Try your hands at forgiving someone else. You may find it makes a difference in your own life. There is also the possibility you walk in unforgiveness because you do not believe forgiveness has been genuinely extended to you. But one cannot receive that which he cannot give and cannot give that which he cannot receive. In life, we must ask for forgiveness for our trespasses against others. We must grant forgiveness when an-other who has trespassed against us seeks forgiveness. We must also learn to receive the forgiveness of others. Factually speaking, however, since forgiveness is more about its impact on the one extending forgiveness it is more important that you focus on forgiving rather than on whether or not someone else has extended a hand of forgiveness to you.

Forgiveness is complicated by a lack of belief, and our belief system is compromised by the fact we find it problematic to trust. We fail to trust because we walk in fear. Fear stymies, stifles, and strangles to the point of cutting off an important life source—others. Take time right now to think about your own life and your forgiveness barometer and remember what follows.

MEDITATION CHALLENGE: Unforgiveness is an "expensive" proposition because of its damaging impact on relationships and community. What is more, unforgiveness is damaging in all of its forms. Essentially, there are three categories of forgiveness: (1) forgiveness between humanity and her God, (2) forgiveness between two or more humans, and (3) forgiveness between human and self. A healthy practice of all three is life altering. Remember you cannot give what you cannot receive, and you cannot receive what you cannot give. One does not change to merit forgiveness; rather, receiving unmerited forgiveness paves the way for healthy transformation. Think about the three forms of forgiveness and how they are exercised in your life. Think of one person in particular from whom you should seek forgiveness. Thereafter, develop courage, and ask this question: Would you forgive me? Then think of another person you need to forgive. Forgive them whether or not they have asked for forgiveness.

— — — —

The next time you are tempted to walk in unforgiveness remember it costs too much. Consequently, here is some practical advice on ways of addressing unforgiveness in your own walk as a leader:

1. Replace the negative with the positive.

2. Change your circle of friends.

3. Change your negative talk.

4. Place positive reminders all over your house.

Meditation 10   ***ENCOURAGEMENT***

Don't Be Discouraged

And David was greatly distressed;
for the people spake of stoning him,
because the soul of all the people was grieved,
every man for his sons and for his daughters:
but David encouraged himself in the Lord his God.
(1 SAMUEL 30:6, KJV)

You need to be aware of what others are doing,
applaud their efforts, acknowledge their successes,
and encourage them in their pursuits.
When we all help one another, everybody wins.
—JIM STOVALL

Correction does much, but encouragement does more.
—JOHANN WOLFGANG VON GOETHE

Today it seems discouragement has become an all too common phenomenon. In fact, we see the evidence of discouragement all around us in the world. From the increase in shootings and murders in major metropolitan areas and in our schools, to the increase in terrorism and attacks in our colleges and universities and around the world, to rising gas and food prices, falling paychecks, layoffs, the housing crisis, to failed businesses and you name it, discouragement is all around us. To make matters worse, it has now become more commonplace than ever before to see or become, even as a leader, one of the discouraged. Discouragement, however, is not our friend, and for many the question is not if you become discouraged but when you become discouraged what are you prepared to do to change your reality? Have you yet reached a point of discouragement in your journey?

To be discouraged means "deprived of courage, hope or confidence, obstructed by opposition or difficulty; hindered."

Let me share what I have learned about the verb discouraged: Discouragement is the palace of the enemy, and the enemy is anyone or anything that would prevent you from reaching your leadership destiny. In the enemy's palace, he houses his friends—hopeless and fearful. And the enemy understands if he can keep you discouraged, then he can send in his friends hopeless and fearful to take you out of the game. Be encouraged because discouraged can be defeated.

Thankfully courage is the enemy of discouragement. Courage allows you to combat fear, which is the precise reason your enemy does not want you to possess courage. Rather, your enemy wants you to be discouraged because when you are discouraged you become paralyzed, and when you are paralyzed you do not do what is needful of you in order to grow and change your circumstances. The truth is you must develop the courage to stare your enemy in the face, call him the lie that he is, and move from the seat of discouragement toward that to which life has called you.

From where is genuine courage derived? For me, it comes

from an intimate relationship with my God. Intimacy with your God can help you overcome the fears of life and allow you to face them with courage. Courage will also assist you in not becoming overly concerned with the dark places in life. It will help you understand there are twenty-four hours in a day, which means the sun will shine again.

In 1 Samuel 30:1–6, it is recorded that when the men of David's army threatened to stone him because the women and children had been taken into captivity, David encouraged himself in his God. The same is true for you. When you find yourself facing discouragement, you must find a source of encouragement. Perhaps your source of encouragement is not the same as mine. Nevertheless, it is incumbent upon each of us to know or have a source of encouragement. Sometimes it will be necessary to encourage yourself. However, when you do encourage yourself, you must have something in which you genuinely believe, and it must be something outside of you and greater than you. It must be a source that is capable of helping to restore you and restore your sense of courage.

As you read this meditation, do you have places in your life wherein you are walking in discouragement? Have you had an experience that has shattered your confidence? Has some obstacle been placed in your pathway that has hindered you from achieving what you believe is within your reach? If so, it is time for encouragement.

MEDITATION CHALLENGE: The next time you feel discouragement rearing its ugly head, challenge yourself to immediately turn your discouragement into encouragement. Write down ten reasons you have to be encouraged, and rehearse them over and over again. Pick up a journal and write down the top fifteen reasons why you are grateful for where you are in life. After you have done those things, find a cause that involves serving those who are less fortunate. You will find that even when you cannot fully encourage yourself, serving others has a unique way of restoring encouragement and its close partner courage.

— — — —

The next time you are tempted to allow discouragement to overtake you, find a quiet place and put your mind to work not only encouraging yourself but also developing a strategy to move you from that place to higher ground. Go back to the formation principles and the elements of the Power Triad. Examine how you might bring them to life in your journey. Implement the SAAG (Setting and Achieving Goals) principle and follow your strategy one day at a time until you are completely lifted from that place. Along the way, remember life will not always be as we desire, but if you can look up you can get up.

Meditation 11   ***WISDOM***

The Honor of Walking in Wisdom

Words spoken by the wise bring them favor,
but the lips of fools consume them.
(ECCLESIASTES 10:12, NRSV)

To conquer fear is the beginning of wisdom.
—BERTRAND RUSSELL

You can buy education but wisdom is a gift from God.
—AUTHOR UNKNOWN

Wisdom is an attribute that many believe comes with age and experience. While it is true untold numbers of individuals find wisdom as they mature in life, there are those who are said to be wise beyond their years. In which category do you believe you fall? Have you experienced the gift of wisdom in your youth, or are you more mature and just settling into your capacity to employ wisdom? The truth is it really does not matter where you fall, for as leaders we all have maturing to do. The more important question to be considered relates to *how* you as a leader will obtain wisdom and begin to exercise wisdom before your days of leadership begin moving toward decline?

Before you can understand what it means to walk in

wisdom, however, you must realize the difference between knowledge and wisdom. Many a leader has overlooked these important distinctions while simultaneously impacting their leadership footprint in a not so positive direction. Knowledge is about knowing. Wisdom, on the other hand, is about knowing what to do. It is one thing to be educated and to know your craft but quite another to know how, when, and where to put your knowledge to use. Although both knowledge and wisdom are great attributes, they are different. Knowledge confirms intellectual capacity, but wisdom proves superior judgment. Wisdom helps you to make prudent decisions under tough circumstances. It aids you to respond in love to difficult situations and sometimes difficult people. For my corporate friends, wisdom in essence is emotional intelligence, and emotional intelligence relates to one's ability to self-regulate his or her emotions or as I have so often heard "to look before you leap" or "think before you speak."

Is your ability to exercise wisdom tested by your role as leader? Are you right now facing a challenge that causes you to question your ability to walk in wisdom? Your ability to walk in wisdom is driven by your capacity to make judicious decisions. Your capacity to walk judiciously is closely tied to a willingness to be intentional about your journey in leadership. To move intentionally requires consistent self-awareness, self-examination, and self-development. It likewise requires that you understand leadership as we have discussed is relational, connectional, and sacrificial and is not advanced by the number of people you encounter; rather, its power is in the depth of the transaction! Moreover, genuinely connected leadership nurtures the possibility that my interrelatedness to an-other allows us to inspire the best in one another. More importantly, connection is the antithesis of envy and strife. Thus, to reach the mark of authentic, connectional leadership necessitates a true ability to walk in harmony with others regulating our interactions in ways that are life-giving and nurturing to an-other. In essence, it takes relationship to the next level. Further, it is sacrificial in that a leader knows the strength of his contribution to others is in the sacrifice he is willing to make on behalf of an-other. These are elements of wisdom important in a journey in leadership.

MEDITATION CHALLENGE: Have you ever considered where you are on the journey to obtaining and walking in wisdom? If not, perhaps the question is appropriately posed for such a time as this in your life. Give some serious thought and consideration to how you have walked as a leader in relation to yourself and others. In doing so, think of three situations where you clearly used wise judgment. Thereafter, consider three situations where you could have exercised an increased level of wisdom. Commit to writing what you could or should have done differently in the second set of examples. Additionally, commit to writing how you will utilize what you did wisely in the first three examples in your leadership going forward.

— — — —

Wisdom is an important aspect of your leadership journey. Do not allow yourself to avoid wisdom; rather, look for ways to obtain and exercise wisdom in all that you do in the name of leadership.

Meditation 12　　　　　　　　***ENDURANCE***

Don't Be Weary in Well-Doing

And let us not grow weary while doing good, for in
due season we shall reap if we do not lose heart.
(GALATIANS 6:9, NKJV)

Rest when you're weary. Refresh and renew
yourself, your body, your mind, your spirit.
Then get back to work.
—RALPH MARSTON

At some point in life most of us are tempted to become weary in well-doing. The weary temptation may be especially true in the lives of those who have given unselfishly in a life of service to others. You might want to know how long it will take before you experience the breakthrough that you have been seeking. Despite the temptation, you must hold fast and not give in to the weariness temptation. It is true we reap what we sow, and it is more blessed to give than to receive.

Perhaps it is time for those of us who are known by the title leader to view giving and serving through a different lens. Instead of looking at giving from the perspective of how much we are blessing someone else through our gift, it might be more fruitful to consider the ability to give as a gift itself. If we look at giving as a gift to the giver as opposed to a gift to the receiver, it will transform our thinking about the value in giving or the value in doing good.

I am not sure about you but I am always thrilled when I receive a gift. The question to consider in this meditation, however, is what would happen if leaders experienced the same or an even greater thrill from giving or living in service to others? As I imagine it, it would be akin to viewing the glass as half full instead of half empty. It would be akin to transforming the source of our joy. After all, transforming our source of joy could very well lead to a greater sense of gratitude.

A NEW CHALLENGE: You are probably looking for more and waiting for your written meditation challenge in this final meditation. While I could provide you with such, I decided instead to prompt you to think more on your own about what endurance means in your life and to create your own challenge. Think about how you would challenge yourself or others you lead to avoid becoming weary in well-doing. After serious contemplation and completing the meditation challenge, think about how you will meet the challenge in your life. Once you have done so, exercise courage and issue the challenge to those you lead.

Chapter 8

THE LAST WORD!

A llow me to close in full lawyer regalia. In a litigated case, it is customary for the judge to allow the attorneys to conclude with a summation, or closing statement. The closing statement is not given the weight of evidence. However, the closing serves as one last opportunity for an attorney to speak to her audience (jury) prior to deliberations. Truthfully, while the closing statement is not evidence, summations have been known to persuade. As I close this work, I would simply like to share a few additional thoughts by way of a "closing statement."

As a result of writing this book, I can say with certainty I am changed. I am not the person I was when I started on this journey. Rewriting the definition of leadership is one clear example. Looking back, this journey began many years ago—long before I had any conscious idea this writing would be part of my journey. I am not the same person I was ten years ago, five years ago, three years ago, two weeks ago, or even one hour ago. Many things have transpired. Most critical, my faith has increased. My determination has increased. My yearning to be a better human being has grown. My skill as a writer has been enlarged. My ability as a critical thinker has been further developed. My ability to lead well has been augmented. In fact, my understanding of who I am authentically and who life has called me to be has become exceedingly clear. I am not the same.

I am proud to say in all my years of living, learning, growing, developing, shaping, becoming, and transforming, I have reached formation. Today, I possess the values and character that represent the best of my mother, the best of my father, and the greatest efforts of becoming the best of who God ordained me to be—a testament to the power of intergenerational leadership.

My desire for you is that you also are not the same. I hope you now have a clearer picture of what you will do with the remainder of your leadership dash. I trust you have spent some time understanding formation and its importance in your leadership journey. I encourage you on your journey toward becoming the best of who you are intended to be. That is the kind of formation that lends access to the great and creates legacy and a pathway for others to reach the same. Moreover, I hope you have a clearer picture of the values and attributes that are critical in great leadership, and I hope they are now even more prominent in your walk as leader.

I am more than optimistic that you are prepared to begin or continue on your journey of turning mere leadership into legacy. In all honesty, you will need to commit to letting some things go while simultaneously agreeing to take on the new. You must be willing to abandon comfort and take up a risk or two. Most important, it is essential for you to embrace a posture of more critical thinking followed by more critical action. I pray this writing has helped you understand the difference between talking and taking action.

In my many years as a practicing attorney and litigator, I learned just how important having the last word is for so many. You name it, and someone desires to have the last word. In politics, in business, in litigation, in theological debate, in medicine, in sports, in newswriting, in familial relationships, and especially marriages, someone always gets the last say. Moreover, many leaders believe they either have the last word or the rights to the last word. And having the last word often means someone wins and someone loses. While having the last word has its perks, having the last word does not always bring the desired results. Great leaders are after great results, and they understand the difference between a post script (p.s.) and a problem solved (p.s.). A post script is any addition or supplement added after the conclusion. It is, in effect, the last word. It does not necessarily denote a solution or resolution. It is simply the last word. But great leaders understand it is significantly more important to solve a problem than to have the last word.

We have learned to be critical thinkers but not critical problem solvers. We spend far too much of our critical thinking time discussing problems, being critical of others, and thwarting progress instead of creating solutions. Great leaders seek solutions and problem solve through leadership that begins with intention, authenticity, transparency, moral and ethical influence, and sustainable impact. Think of it like this: Life is a canvas, and true leaders are artists. Each day you are given an opportunity to paint a portion of your masterpiece. Are you using your leadership dash to create the masterpiece you were intended to create? I pray this work has helped you begin or continue painting your strokes while simultaneously looking for the lessons in your life experiences. Remember, experience is life's best instructor.

Now before officially concluding, I would like to share one last experience in which I believe there are great lessons. On Saturday morning, September 18, 2010, I left my home for my usual a.m. walk. On this particular morning my plan was to walk five miles, which would have translated into walking two and one-half miles from my home and two and one-half miles on the return back home. I was also planning to use the recording device on my cell phone to record some things I had wanted to write for quite some time. So I started on my walk and began recording. When I looked up, I was four miles from home. This meant I had four miles to go in the other direction in order to return home. I looked into the sky and noticed it had become as dark as an early evening sky. It was overcast, and I saw dark clouds that suggested it was about to storm. So I turned and headed in the direction of home. As I was walking, I sent a text to my best friend to say it is about to pour rain, and I was more than thirty minutes from home. I walked a little farther and indeed the rain came. The more I walked, the more it rained. I thought to myself that I couldn't run because I did not think my knees could withstand a run similar to those of years gone by. So I kept walking. I walked by a gas station and thought perhaps I would duck inside and wait until the rain passed. But I decided otherwise because to do so would not move me any closer to my goal: home. I started to think about things like my hair and getting soaked from the rain.

But as the rain began to come down even heavier, I decided to look for the lesson in the experience instead of focusing on all that was going wrong at that moment. I said to myself that the only way to know whether or not my knees would withstand a jog was to actually try it. I then began jogging, and I surprised myself at how far I was able to run. During my run, it got even darker outside. The rain came at an even heavier pace, and it began to thunder followed by lightning. Even though I was getting soaked and wanted to give up, I kept jogging while telling myself I can do this. I was surprised because my knees were still not hurting. So I kept on jogging, sometimes at a pace that was similar to a very fast walk, but I kept jogging until finally I reached my goal: home.

The lesson I learned in my experience on September

18 had many components: (1) I learned I can do anything to which I put my mind. (2) I learned that sometimes in life we get caught off guard by rain and even storms. But I also learned as a leader it is incumbent upon me not to give up in the rain or the storm and not to doubt what I can accomplish all the while moving in the direction of my goal. When I walked into the door of my home, it was clear to me I had actually broken through a finish line. If I could break through the finish line of a jog several miles from home when I thought my running days were over, I could do anything to which I put my mind. (I haven't jogged seriously in at least five years.) It then became imminently clear to me there is a force outside of you that will allow you to do exceeding and abundantly above all you could ask or think. So I close with a simple question: What finish line are you seeking to break through? Be encouraged, and use the lessons in this book to help you break through your finish line on your leadership dash.

Aim for 100 because 99½ won't do!

CHARTING YOUR LEADERSHIP DASH

CHARTING YOUR LEADERSHIP DASH